CHEATING
THE
DEALER

CLASSIFIED

*Author Reveals
the Top Secrets
to Saving Thousands
On Your Car Repair*

STEVEN E. SHAW

NEW YORK

CHEATING THE DEALER

CLASSIFIED: *Author Reveals the Top Secrets to Saving Thousands On Your Car Repair*

by STEVEN E. SHAW

© 2011 Steven E. Shaw. All rights reserved.

ISBN 978-1-60037- 844-7 (paperback)
Library of Congress Control Number: 2010933636

Published by:

MORGAN JAMES PUBLISHING
The Entrepreneurial Publisher
5 Penn Plaza, 23rd Floor
New York City, New York 10001
(212) 655-5470 Office
(516) 908-4496 Fax
www.MorganJamesPublishing.com

Cover Design by:
Rachel Lopez
Rachel@r2cdesign.com

Interior Design by:
Bonnie Bushman
bbushman@bresnan.net

CHEATING THE DEALER

A Top Secret look from the inside
to saving $1000's on your auto repair

TABLE OF
TOP SECRETS

INTRODUCTION

Imagine walking into a gleaming car dealership and being taken aback by the wonder of it all. Truly envision those new cars on the showroom floor. Picture that Mustang convertible sitting in the center of the marble tiled floor. Just visualize the little, red Chevrolet Corvette. Maybe a Ferrari Dealership -- dream of that bright, red 430 Ferrari Spider with black interior with red, hand stitched trim and just a touch of accent to make you know how fast this car can go. Breathe…Ahhh… the scent of the brand new leather seats… Breathe again. Smell the aroma of a room packed with new cars and the rubber of those Goodyear tires. The taste of money permeates the entire place. Whose money? Your money!

You are here to get the car of your dreams. Before you even walk in, you are fantasizing about driving down the Pacific Coast Highway, or Main Street of your hometown. You dream of yourself winding down the road, hugging the curves, your fantasy date (or your spouse) by your side with your hair blowing in the breeze. Feel the wind and hear your radio as it drowns out all of your cares. Crank up your favorite tunes and make this your ultimate road trip. You are in love with your new car. You are now going to make your dream a reality and go get that sweet ride!

You suffered through the purchase process. You made the purchase! You're even more in love with yourself. You outsmarted the car guys and have your baby.

Now…

You go by the neighbors' house. You must show off this prize. You drive everywhere!

The first day that you buy your new car is the only time errands are fun. You park your new love in the furthest parking spot from the entrance. As you walk to the entrance you turn around at least 10 times just to admire her. Nah, you are really admiring yourself. Congratulations, you outsmarted that car salesman. You stole this one. This time it's going to be different. There will be no scratches, dents or dings – EVER. This amazing piece of machinery was hand built just for you.

And you live happily ever after?

Not always.

Sorry, but it's time to WAKE UP! Wake up from your daydream. Of course, the darn thing breaks down! Of course it breaks down at the worst time too.

Now what?

What do you do? This is when the proverbial rubber meets the road. Open the glove box, find the service guy and call ahead for your appointment. That is if the dealership introduced you to the service guy already. That is if you bought the car from your hometown dealer. Or were you the one who outsmarted everyone and drove miles out of your way to save a few bucks? Maybe does not seem so smart now?

So you finally get your magical time slot to meet the car guys, the so-called "doctor" of the car. Anxiety is probably what you feel as you drive your brand new car into the service department. Why, anxiety? Because you think you are about to get ripped off! There they are, the service guys just standing there waiting to rip you off. What will they try to sell me? YOU THINK: "I just want them to fix my car!"

Kind of blows your mind doesn't it? I am here to tell you it does not have to be overwhelming. With just a little knowledge and some inside tips or *Top Secrets* you can outsmart the service guy all day long.

Do not believe the guy behind the service desk is the former auto mechanic or just a good guy hired to take care of you. He is a salesman. He gets paid to take care of your car. In a well-managed dealership, he is professional. He is a service consultant. His job is to keep you informed of your needs. These needs do include selling you things for your car. Most service people get paid a lot to sell. Believe me; I pay my service salespeople very well. When you come in for an oil change and tire rotation, I want you to be prepared for certain things. Items like flushes, fluid exchange, tires, brakes, spark plugs, gaskets, rods, pistons and maybe a valve or two, the dealer maintenance package and the manufacturer recommended packaged services are on the menu for your money. What is a flush anyway? What the heck is a U-Joint service and when do you need it?

I am going to tell you what to buy and what to stay away from. I will reveal the ins and outs of the maintenance game and you will walk away from this read an educated consumer. You will have your own masters' degree in saving money.

Or as I call it;

CHEATING THE DEALER.

1

THE PROBLEM WITH DEALERSHIPS

I don't know ONE person who doesn't get nervous or think they are about to be cheated, when they hear the word CAR DEALERSHIP. The problem: lack of trust. Consumers are weary of dealerships because they have been trained to distrust them. The aftermarket world and media has portrayed the new car dealership as the big bad wolf. In addition to this stereotypical media-marketing program, the reality is that the new car dealership is not easily understood. From the outside, it appears as if the dealership is a place where consumers are looked down upon and a place where consumers get treated poorly and taken advantage of upon arrival. Consumers ASSUME they are going to get ripped off the moment they walk in the door.

Owners of dealerships love their cars. To many dealers, it is like their own private museum. But, do car dealers want to sell cars? The answer is yes. Over the years, car dealerships have built a reputation for being awfully proud of their inventory and only want to sell it to the most qualified buyer. Forget about the guy who has had tough time in life. Oh, and the guy with bad credit? HA. Get ready to be treated as second-class citizen if you have bad credit.

Because of all these riddles, most of the time, as buyers, we start lying through our teeth the moment we get on the dealership lot. First we say we are just looking. The salesman replies with his answers and tries to get us into a conversation. We do everything to make the salesperson think we really do not want the car. After an exhausting back and forth, back and forth, back and forth, "conversation" we go on a road test, and then finally we decide this is the car we are interested in purchasing! WOHOO. Over? Hardly. Now comes the hard part; the negotiation of the purchase deal. Both sides begin posturing for the best deal or most profit won or saved on the car. It is a grueling process. Then at last the deal is made. Now comes the finance part. Finally, to finish, we drive out with the car we wanted. This stressful process can take hours upon hours.

Going through every emotion is not uncommon. We get excited to see the cars, thrilled to choose our personal statement or the four wheel identity of who we are. But, then we become angry at the deal making process. We sometimes get sad when it looks as if the deal is not going to happen. Then when we think all is lost, the salesman states, "Congratulation - we have a deal". Next is bewilderment, we then question if there actually was a better deal to be had. We always query ourselves and think as if we actually got ripped off. The answer is really, who knows? Only the dealership sales manager knows exactly.

There are no college classes on buying a car. Oh sure you can get a book for "dummies" on purchasing your new vehicle. Just try those techniques when you walk in the door. The dealership is wiser than you are. The dealership has the car you want. You try and do your best to get the deal you want and pay the payment you need. There is an art to buying and selling cars. Most of the time buyers are just happy to be approved on the deal! If we get near the payment we want, we are even more excited.

There are books and Internet sites that can guide you on the path to a great deal. You will never really know if there was any more money on the table, thus a mystery is created not to mention a subliminal message that the dealer may just have taken more of your money than he needed. Or, maybe you could have worked it for just a few less dollars. Many times we just are not sure. Again this creates a distrustful situation. So now when the deal is complete; the moment you get into your new car, you cannot help but harbor some anxiety towards that dealership.

Now when you finally made your purchase and made it through that hurricane, what happens when you have a service issue? Most of the time it is a crapshoot at best on how to get the vehicle repaired. I went through graduate school and I have an MBA in business management; did anyone tell me how to understand auto repair? The answer is NO!

No one teaches us how to understand what the lights on the dashboard are telling us. It seems as if the auto manufacturers try hard to keep their technology secret. I studied for four years and have an "Advanced Technical Degree" in Automotive

Technology and it is nearly impossible for me to keep up with the changes occurring daily in the automotive field.

Cars have become so advanced today. Computers talk to computers in your car. There is the body computer talking with the electronic light computer. They both talk to the engine control computer. All the computers report to the main computer. Some cars have over 500 computers in the car. I heard recently that the high performance cars have a computer that controls the spoiler on the rear deck lid. They communicate through fiber optic wires. Did you know that some cars have radar? Some cars can keep you at a certain distance from the vehicle in front of you. Some cars have lane-changing assist. Recently, I saw a show where some Audi cars were driving themselves.

Dealerships spend hundreds of thousands of dollars on diagnostic equipment each year to ensure they can interpret the data stored on these computer machines. How in the world are you expected to understand and keep up with this technology as a consumer? As a retail consumer you already work a full time job and sometimes two. Your wife or husband works to maintain your own household. After spending a significant amount of your hard earned money just to purchase the car, now you have to learn auto repair. It is not really fair. It is, however, life, as we know it. *Cheating the Dealer* will arm you with the top secrets to overcoming this unfairness. *Cheating the Dealer* is going to give you the secrets to saving money while utilizing the dealership's own staff for your benefit.

SO WHY DID I WRITE THIS BOOK? TO ENSURE I WOULD NEVER WORK AT A DEALERSHIP AGAIN? HARLDY! I WANT YOU TO UNDERSTAND HOW THE DEALERSHIP WORKS. I WANT YOU IN MY SERVICE DEPARTMENTS. I WANT YOU TO BE AN EDUCATED CONSUMER AND SAVE BIG BUCKS HAVING YOUR CAR SERVICED.

I have spent most of my career as a director and consultant at a new car dealership. Through education, experience and on the job training, I developed my own style and purpose. I created my program that I successfully teach and train at dealerships.

I learned many years ago that people love their cars. When cars break, people sometimes break too. Can you blame them? The automobile is typically the consumer's 2nd if not 1st largest purchase in their lifetime. Not only the monetary significance of the purchase, is it widely understood that most people identify with their cars. Many times, the car is a representation of our personalities.

Cars are one of the most valued possessions we have. But the hard reality of it is, whoever the driver, at that moment when the car breaks down, that situation takes over our lives. It instantaneously becomes the single most important crisis.

Good car people recognize this simple truth. *The business is about people more than cars. It is easy to "fix cars" – "fixing people" is the key to any car dealership success.* And with this knowledge, I take my position seriously. As a service manager and consultant in the car business, I can think of no other job as rewarding as what I do. Yeah I am sure there is plenty of more important work to be done, doctors, lawyers, brokers, hell the President of the United States, but fixing people in their time of need ranks right up at the top. Especially, when the chips are down, even the really important people need their cars fixed.

I teach and train service advisors and managers in the business how to be great sales people. I teach my peers how to make you so happy that you want to spend money on your cars. I have never once sold a customer something that their car did not need. I will never teach anyone to sell anything that is not above board and necessary for the repair, upkeep or maintenance of the car.

I want you to know there are great men and women in the car business; however I am going to arm you for the worst while looking for the best in them and the best of them.

When you are done reading *Cheating The Dealer*, I want you to be able to fully understand and be able to ask the dealership questions like these:

- Can you itemize my repairs with parts and labor listed **separately**?

- Can you offer me a free courtesy inspection (or World class Inspection™) with my repairs today?

- Can you please review my repair order with me before I leave so I thoroughly understand what repairs are being looked at today?

- Can you please facebook or twitter me at the time convenient for me so that we can review the work that is necessary.

- Can you provide me alternate transportation while my vehicle is being serviced?

- Can you call me at a time convenient for me so we can review the work that is necessary?

- Can you please explain the technical jargon in my language so I will understand the work that needs to be performed?

- Can you please give me an accurate promise time when the car will be completed?

- Can you please review the final charges of my repair order to ensure that they are what I authorized?

- Can you wash my car so it looks as if I just left a new car dealership?

As a consumer you understand that the business of buying and servicing a car is not about the car itself. It is about the relationship with the salesperson and the service person. Consumers have the ability to choose where to buy and where to service the car. Dealerships have just done a poor job in the past of getting the message out that they provide a better service to the customer than everyone else. Dealerships have lost the battle about customer service and prices in the marketing and media arena. It is time to change all that.

Now it is time to understand how a dealership really operates...so you can CHEAT THE DEALER.

2

THE DEALERSHIP EXPLAINED

As you will find throughout this book, car dealerships and the people who work there are pretty simple. You know the saying about how simple men are? That all men need is to eat, drink and sleep? It's the same for a car dealership. All they need to do is sell, sell, and sell. Nearly every position in the automotive dealership is a sales position.

It is important to understand that car dealership people are the best sales men and women in the world. A car dealership is a business that has many different businesses inside it. Each business must be profitable. We sell at every opportunity. We learn to make a profit in everything we do, or we just do not do it. The businesses within the dealership are:

- New Car Department – New Car Sales
- Used Car Department –Used Car Sales
- Finance and Insurance Department – Selling Loans, Warranties, Accessories

- Body Shop or Collision Center – Collision Repair Sales
- Parts and Accessories Department – Parts Sales
- Service Department – Repair and Maintenance Sales

NEW CAR, USED CAR, FINANCE DEPARTMENT

Quickly let's break down the businesses or departments. Obviously the new and used car departments sell cars. Although my book is directed to the service consumer, I will give you a couple simple tips on the sales department. Always do your research on the Internet before coming into the dealership to purchase a car. Also, do not feel obligated to purchase anything when you walk in. Go to the dealership and ask questions. Learn about the car and the financing options before you sit down to negotiate a deal. The first Top Secret I am going to reveal right now. Before you buy a car at any dealership; go interview the service manager.

TOP SECRET

Before you buy a car at any dealership, go and interview the service manager.

You will need to read on to understand this Top Secret tip. The service manager is going to give you more information than any other person in the entire dealership. Before you complete this read you will understand how important this Top Secret tip is for you.

The finance department does the paperwork and gets you a loan. The finance department is where you purchase extended warranties, as well. The finance department is another business inside the dealership. The finance department makes money by getting you a loan. They also are entitled to make certain monies on the sale of your extended service contract. Many times the finance department sells you accessories, radios, ground effects kits and other items like running boards and rims. Always remember my favorite line…"we are a dealership, let's make a deal". Ask for a discount. Ask for the price you can afford. If you are not good at negotiating, take a friend with you to make sure you get the best price. The best advice I can give is to be a fully educated consumer. Research your options. It will pay off for you.

THE BODY SHOP

The body shop fixes your car in a collision. Although many dealerships still have body shops, others are getting away from collision repair. This industry is more in the hands of the insurance companies now. Body shops are becoming very highly specialized. It takes a very sophisticated operator to run this business. Many dealers are choosing to stay away from this business for that reason and prefer to partner with a local reputable collision center to support their efforts. If your car is in an accident look for a "certified" body shop from the manufacturer of your vehicle. Call the dealership and they can usually refer you to the most competent shop in your area.

THE PARTS DEPARTMENT

The parts business or department is just that: PARTS. The parts department is tasked with stocking an inventory of parts to fix almost any car that comes thru the door. This too takes a very savvy business man or manager to keep track of the thousands of parts and part numbers for all of the nuts, bolts, doors, hoods, brakes, engines, transmissions and every single clip that keeps your car running. It is almost impossible to understand and stock every part for every year since inception that the car was made. The parts manager at a car dealership must have a brain the size of Montana to understand all these numbers. Or he just has a very sophisticated computer. The dealership parts manager is a master of parts inventory.

THE MYSTERIOUS
SERVICE DEPARTMENT...

Now the service department is probably one of the strangest places on earth. What makes this place so mysterious is actually really simple. The service department sells time. What's that you say? It sells time. The service department is tasked with selling the labor time of all the mechanics in the department. The more mechanics or technicians as we call them now, the more labor time we can sell. And our job is to keep them busy all day long.

Selling labor time is not like selling anything else. Let me try to explain. If I have a part on the shelf and it does not sell, we can still sell that part tomorrow. The part is still here and available. If a mechanic is not working on something, or not fixing something, his time is idle and his labor time is not sold. The dealership service department loses that time to sell. This is extremely important to understand. Imagine that jug of milk in your refrigerator. The expiration date is tomorrow morning. At midnight tonight the milk expires. I better drink it all, or it's no good. A technician's time is like that only to the extreme. His time expires immediately as time passes. So for each passing moment he is idle, the time cannot be made up. That time is lost, just like the milk. But you say he can work a little harder tomorrow. True, but he could do that anyway. The time idle is the time lost forever.

THE FLAT RATE SYSTEM

Now even more importantly, technicians at almost every single car dealership in the country work on a system called "flat rate". Some call it piecework. Here is how it works:

The auto manufacturer calculates how long it should take to perform a repair and posts this into a manual. This manual is called a labor time guide. When a repair is to be performed, someone, usually a service advisor looks up the time necessary to perform this task. He then calculates the labor time and the labor rate. He multiplies those together, and then adds the parts price and then gives you a total for the repair. It sounds simple. Usually it is.

Mechanics are very smart people. They learn and adapt. They think well about cars, electricity and mechanical things. They are mechanically inclined. And like most smart people, once they do things a few times they get really good. However, if they finish the repair faster than the book says it should take, well the mechanic wins. And technically you win as well. You still pay the same amount but your car gets done faster than promised.

Sounds great?

Nope, sounds like a rip-off. "I am confused? I get my car done faster than promised but I still pay the same"?

Exactly!

On the other hand, if it takes a mechanic longer than the book says, you still pay the same. The dealership loses, the mechanic loses and you win. You still pay the same amount as you agreed upon.

Once you have agreed to the price. The price is the price.

THE PEOPLE IN THE DEALERSHIP

The service department is an intertwined mix of people and process. Talk about adding to the confusion and mystery of the dealership.

When you drive into the dealership parking lot, look for the arrows or signs that direct you to the Service Drive. The service driveway, or "drive" for short, is the place where you will find most of the customer activity within the service department. Most dealerships have a service drive. Customers just pull as far into the dealership driveway or garage that he or she has access to and usually a service person will greet the customer or at least direct him to the correct location to park the vehicle.

When you first drive in you will most likely see people working in the service driveway or the "write up area".

This is where customer concerns will be written down and a "Repair Order" or "Work Order" created. The person that will greet you is a service advisor and will take your concerns and write them down on a Repair Order so that a technician understands and can correctly fix your vehicle.

The service advisor should be knowledgeable about your particular type of car or truck and therefore be able to advise you of the proper maintenance and repairs on your vehicle. They should also keep you informed of any manufacture recalls. This is all in a maximum effort to maintain your vehicle at the highest performance.

TOP SECRET

*The service guys and gals that you
meet on the drive are sales people.*

It is also critical to understand that these service people are service **sales** people. Sometimes they have other titles, service consultants, service team leaders, assistant service managers, or just about any clever name to make you feel good about them. Just remember they are sales people.

To recap: the service advisor is the front line guy. The service advisor is the person you meet when you drive in the dealership. He is the person that will make or break your experience. He is usually paid on commission. Most of the time his commission is based upon what you spend, meaning what he sells you. He is also paid for your satisfaction. Always be thinking that he lives or dies on your satisfaction. The service advisor reports to the service manger.

TOP SECRET

The service advisor lives and dies on your satisfaction.

THE SERVICE MANAGER

The service manager is usually the highest on the food chain in the department. Typically he has a technical background and can explain the ins and outs of your car to you in a language that you can understand. The service manager reports to the service director or directly to the General Manager or Dealer Owner.

In larger organizations there may be a service director. This person is usually in a position of authority to make decisions on behalf of the dealer owner.

THE GENERAL MANAGER

Usually above the service manager is the General Manager. The GM. This is the individual who runs the store and oversees everyone in both service and sales. He reports only to the Dealer Principal or the corporation that owns the company. Most General Managers wear quite a few hats. They are responsible for everyone in the store including the customers and they also have the ultimate responsibility for profit and loss. They are the best sales people and businessmen and women for that reason. Most do love customers; love being involved and love being profitable.

THE DEALER PRINCIPAL

The Dealer Principal is the owner of the franchise. He is the ultimate authority in the organization. His name is on the sign.

In the modern era of new car dealerships, corporations are now purchasing dealerships. Wall Street has figured out that dealerships can be profitable ventures. There are publicly held companies who own dealerships. An example of this is Auto Nation. There are others that are well-established corporations holding car dealership including Sonic Corporation (not the burger joint.) or Lithia Motors. You might even own stock in a dealership group as a part of your own investment portfolio.

The importance of these auto groups for consumers to know is simple; they want and need your business to be successful. No different than a single owner franchise, they are well-funded companies that provide an important service to the community and now the country. They do provide jobs and tax revenue to our cities and states. If you want to find out that a corporation owns your local dealership, do your research. All of their information is available. In these organizations, the GM is the usually the person in charge of the store. He or she is the person to get to. And sometimes through your research on line you can find customer assistance for the big groups. My advice is to stay with the person at the local level if at all possible.

TOP SECRET

Want to know something, call the receptionist, she will tell you everything.

If you want to know who owns the place or who is in charge, call the main phone number and ask the receptionist. She will tell you anything you want to know.

YOUR CAR DOC

Let's not forget the technicians. Having worked in many car dealerships, I have met some very intelligent men and women. Those people out there in the "back" of the dealership are pretty smart. Most do not have a college education from an Ivy League school, let alone any university. But do not be fooled, what they lack in business training they make up for it in a highly specialized area; the mechanics of your car.

Most technicians or mechanics have dedicated their professional lives to auto repair. They simply love what they do. They spend eight hours each day diagnosing and repairing cars like yours. They also go to school for hundreds of hours each year. They are the ones that must diagnosis your car in a timely manner. They must figure out how to correctly repair your car in the established time. They must do this correctly the first time or you, as a customer, will not be happy with your car. The mechanics in the shop have a tremendous responsibility. As Jack Nicholson said in the movie *A Few Good Men,* "You have the luxury of not knowing what I know" these men study each and every day. I know many that take home service manuals and read at night. This is just like you and I reading a book from our favorite author. Sometimes their favorite author is an engineer at General Motors. I can only imagine what a mechanics wife thinks when a mechanic brings home a wiring diagram and studies it before bed. I am fascinated how someone could love this technical study so well. Believe me when I say; some do!

These mechanics keep us all safe on the road. Our brake systems are computer controlled. Fiber optic wires run through the hidden panels of the car and your dealership mechanics understand how to decipher the data that runs throughout. Spend a few minutes with this person and he just may get invited over some night for dinner. These really are the people keeping us running every day of our lives.

The next time you see a car dealership mechanic walking down the street or at another retail store, give him a hug. Seriously, say thanks for keeping you safe!!!

THE DEALERSHIP SERVICE DEPARTMENT VS. EVERYONE ELSE

Now you know the people who make up the dealership. Most of these men and women are just like you and I. They are good people who are dedicated to making your experience a good one. The dealership offers the consumer many things that an independent shop cannot begin to offer. There are 7 key points.

1. Training

The auto manufacturer trains the dealership mechanics. This means that Ford Motor Company has training facilities specifically designed to train the technicians at Ford Dealerships. If you own a Ford and have it serviced by the dealership, most likely the mechanic that works on your car has Ford Training. This is true for every manufacturer. The manufactures have training programs that are specifically designed to train and educate its technicians on the products they repair and maintain. Not only are technicians trained at the training center, the auto maker has field engineers that routinely visit the dealership to ensure that technicians are up to date on the latest technology. Also, technicians receive daily electronic training via the web. Many vehicles can be updated just like your pc right from the diagnostic equipment. Your car may require software updates from the manufacturer. If you visit the independent shop that technician has no idea of the updates required or available for your car. These repairs are generally FREE.

The manufacture has specific training for each position in the dealership. Most salesmen learn about the product so they can sell you the vehicle. The technicians have technical classes. Service Advisors have specific product training and customer service classed designed to enhance your ownership experience. Many manufactures offer training for the cashier and receptionist as well. Everyone is working to ensure you have a delightful experience at the new car dealership.

I am about to blow your mind. Imagine the auto technician who has worked a Ford Dealership for 20 years. This is quite common in the dealership industry. Did you ever stop to think about how many Ford vehicles he has worked on? Let's go through a quick calculation.

A technician averages 5 cars per day. The technician works 20 days per month. There are 12 months per year. Each year a dealership technician works on 1200 Ford vehicles. Multiply this 1200 vehicles times the number of years at the dealership. We are using 20 years. Twenty years multiplied times 1200 vehicles equals 24,000 Fords.

WOW! Just think about that. Do you think he is qualified to fix your Ford?

Imagine the independent shop technician who probably sees Fords occasionally. Who is more qualified to work on your car? I submit that the dealership technician has the independent technician beat every time.

2. OEM Parts

OEM stands for Original Equipment Manufacturer. The company that makes the original parts for your car makes the replacement parts for your car. If you own a Chevrolet and you visit a Chevrolet Dealer, you will get Chevrolet parts installed during the repairs or maintenance.

Obviously this is the best product for your car. These products meet the original equipment design intent for the vehicle. General Motors, Ford and all the automakers have a division that produces parts. These parts are to replace the original ones on your car.

Many times the manufacturer gives the consumer a one-year warranty on the replacement parts. In the event of a failure of one of these parts, the auto manufacturer also covers the labor to replace this component. As a rule, most aftermarket warranties last only three months long and do not typically cover the labor to replace the parts if they fail. Also, many of the manufactures have a second tier of parts. This means if you do not want the NEW PART, you can have a remanufactured part from the Original Equipment Producer. This part is still a higher quality and designed specifically for your vehicle. Other second tier parts are new however come badged as remanufactured and sold a lesser price. It is almost like getting the generic prescription drug. It is still made exactly as the original with a different name.

3. Equipment and Tools

All cars require special tools to complete some repairs. Many transmissions, engines, radios and other parts have very specialized components. Only the dealership has the exact tools to make these repairs. The aftermarket companies develop this tools overtime but they are just not exactly as the automaker designs. They work too. The just do not work as well as the auto manufactures.

4. Working Capital

The auto manufacturer requires the dealership to have a certain amount of working capital. This means that the dealership must have money in reserve to sustain itself. In other words, most dealerships are financially sound and will be around for a while. Typically new car dealerships do not open one day and close the next. I have seen fly by night repair shops open on Monday and close by Friday duping the vehicle owners out of thousands of dollars.

5. Other Services

Most dealerships offer other services to its owners. These services include items such as free shuttle rides to owner's home and sometimes dealerships offer rental cars while the owner's vehicle is in for repair. Coffee, breakfast, lunch, and boutiques for apparel or toys for kids, manicures, massages and shoe shines are also not uncommon. I know of a Ford Dealership that offers ATM machines and Lottery tickets. Most now have WIFI and business centers. It is important that when you purchase your car that you have a place to wait and visit that is warm and friendly. Most dealerships are leading the world for customer service standards.

6. Manufactures Warranty

The automakers provide your new car with a warranty against defects and performance. This essentially means that if you have a problem caused by a defective part or the performance of a part is below the manufacturer's specification, the auto manufacturer will replace that part at no cost at the dealership. Each dealership is authorized by the manufacturer it represents. For instance, Jeep Corporation authorizes Jeep Dealers. You are eligible to take your (insert make) to any authorized (same make) dealership around the country. Most will only honor the warranty in the United States.

If you are traveling and need repairs; go to the local dealership with your make of vehicle and have the repairs completed. If you are driving outside the country with your vehicle and need repairs, many will not honor the warranty. Some auto manufacturers ask you to pay for the repairs and they will reimburse you through your hometown dealership. They will have you to take your receipts to the dealership and submit a claim for reimbursement.

Read your owners manual for specifics on traveling. Also read your owners manual for the length of time and mileage for your specific vehicle. An example of this warranty would be 3 years or 36,000 miles whichever comes first.

7. Nationwide Parts Warranty

The dealership can offer one more item that even the best of independent shops cannot – Nationwide Warranty. Every part that the dealership replaces comes with a warranty. The vehicle manufacturer backs this warranty. Typically, the term for this warranty is 12 Months or 12,000 Miles. This means even if you are traveling out of state and you have the same repair necessary or the same part fails, YOU ARE COVERED. The parts warranty usually covers the labor to install another part and the part itself. The tow bill should be covered also. If you are stranded out of state on a Sunday, the parts warranty may cover your hotel bill as well. Can your independent shop say that? Can Cousin Billy Bob protect you in an emergency? I doubt it. Call Billy Bob tonight and tell him you car is broken down in Mississippi and see if he can head on over to rescue you? If so, send me an email and I'll write a book about him too. Maybe I'll just hire him.

There is a lot of value in going to a dealership, but when you are thinking of service, you NEED to keep these things in mind… do not become a victim!

AVOIDING SERVICE TRAPS BEFORE YOUR PURCHASE THE CAR.

You are on your way to purchase a car - what should you do?

I actually advise my friends to meet the service team **BEFORE** they buy a car. Eventually you are going to spend time in that service department during the course of the next few years of ownership of the vehicle. Get to know these people immediately. They could become your closest friends. It is much harder to rip off someone you know and care about.

As you learn about your dealership before the purchase, ask the SERVICE TEAM about things like rental cars. Does the selling dealership provide you a loaner vehicle when your car is in for service? Sales people will always tell you that this department provides you a car. Then many times you show up expecting a rental car and the service guy tells you otherwise. This gets the service relationship off to a bad start. Here comes that trust issue. Of course you believe the sales person; he took the time to get to know you. He built a relationship with you and then you bought a car from him. It happens sometimes where that salesman is not even employed at the dealership when you come back for service. You are the one standing there without a ride home.

Ask the service person about maintenance on the car. How much money does an oil change cost? How often should you change the oil on the car? Is it every 3 months or 3000 miles? Or is it every 5 months or 5000 miles? Did you know some cars have annual services now?

I have a friend who purchased a Porsche Boxster. She takes her Porsche to an independent shop for repairs and oil change services. I once asked her for the reason she did not go to the dealer. She stated that she trusted him and his prices were lower than the prices at the dealership. I decided to research this. Come to find out, Porsche Boxster's require an annual service. Some dealerships will perform this service for $199.00. She was paying $99.00 every 3 months for the service. Just doing the math equates to $99 multiplied by 4 times per year equals 396.00 for oil service. Had she taken the car to the dealership she would have saved 196.00 on oil service for the year. And imagine how much her time was worth. I can think of many other things to do each quarter than spend time at a dealership.

Ask the question. How often does my car need service? Save your money.

In the first year of ownership you should not have to pay for anything more than the oil and filter change. Many times you are entitled to a free alignment. Most manufactures will pay for an alignment in the first 6 to 12 months of ownership. I suggest that you ask your service person about alignments. Find out if the manufacturer will pay for one. Ask; "what is the latest interval that you can get this for free?" Then have it done towards the end of that time period. You will extend your tires as a result. Again this is saving more money. As a rule, you should have your alignment checked once per year. So why not wait till the last minute on this and save yourself $100s of dollars.

TOP SECRET

You can get a free alignment
within the first year of ownership.

Most service people will not tell you this unless you ask. Again this is a trust issue. Cheating the Dealer is the only place that will give you this information.

How about towing? Do you know that towing is almost always covered under your warranty? Many people choose to purchase a club membership. This is an unnecessary expense for most consumers after purchasing the vehicle. Almost every vehicle comes with a roadside assistance program. Ask the service team about the roadside assistance program before purchasing the car. You can save a few hundred dollars on car club memberships. It is just a matter of knowing what questions to ask when you purchase the car.

You can also make a deal in the service department. Many of the prices are fixed. These package services are items such as an oil change or a tire rotation. Dealerships have a competitive price on these repairs. However just by asking the question, say, "If I buy four tires, can I get a free alignment?"

Don't be surprised when the service guy says, "Yes."

The store you purchase your car from has a vested interest in your happiness. It always makes me wonder why a consumer will drive all the way across town or 100s of miles away to purchase a car and then drive one block away to have it serviced. Build that relationship from the start. Day one make sure the dealership where you purchase your vehicle takes you back to the service department again and introduces you to the service staff. Get a contact person immediately. You need to know who is working on your car and who to contact in case of trouble.

There are so many more reasons you should go to your dealer…

THE DEALERSHIP SERVICE DEPARTMENT VS. THE INDEPENDENT REPAIR SHOP

Before you get carried away and tell me that you never go to the dealer for repairs, let me tell you a smidge about independent repair shops. If you want to rank the used car sales guy just below an attorney, well keep going down the list until you find the shade tree guy with the certified logo on his sign. Don't get me wrong, there are plenty of honest and trust worthy folks out there trying to make a living fixing your car. How do you know which one of these guys to trust?

Dealership vs. Independent Shop Chart

Dealership VS. Everyone Else	Dealership	Independent Shop	Insert Relative Here
Key Features			
Training	Manufacture Training	3rd Party Training	Not Sure
OEM Parts	Manufacturer Part	3rd Party Parts	Not Sure
Equipment & Tools	Manufacturer Tools	3rd Party Tools	Not a clue
Working Capital	Required Minimum Capital to Operate	No Requirements	Good Luck
Customer Focused	Dealership and Manufacture Based Customer Satisfaction Programs	No Requirements	Beg them to do it!
Manufactures Warranty	Manufacturer Warranty	3rd Party	Help
Nationwide Parts Warranty	Nationwide Parts Warranty	Local to the store	Most likely None
Full Circle Satisfaction	Dedicated Team to ensure satisfaction	No Requirements	Go Away, I did you a favor

How do you know what those person's credentials are? I submit to you that it may be impossible to know for certain what certifications a mechanic really has. At a dealership, the manufacturer certifies that the technician working in the shop has had the training. If you see the certificate, it is most likely accurate.

What is the labor rate he is charging you? Many times, the independent shop is not any cheaper than the dealer. It is your perception that the independent shop is JUST CHEAPER. The independent shop does not have to post a labor rate. I know many independent shops that charge as much, or more, than the dealer. I have a close friend who owns a muffler / tune up shop. His rate is $30 per hour more that most dealers in his neighborhood. I am happy for him that he can charge and customers pay the rate. He runs a first class shop. I know his mechanics are not factory trained. I also know his overhead is lower than the dealership.

Why would a customer pay more than the dealership for labor and parts when the original equipment is less expensive?

The answer is SHOCKING! NO trust. The dealership has done a poor job of educating the consumer of the qualities and performance levels of the dealership service department.

Ask yourself this question, is all that you want a cheaper price? Or do you want the peace of mind that goes along with the dealership service? Do the independent shops go to training specifically for your make of car? Do the independent shops use the factory recommended parts designed for your make and model of car. No and No. Do the independents get the support from the manufacturer that is necessary to maintain the highest quality standards on your second and sometimes your largest investment? I don't think so! So what can you do? Maybe you can call your relative who is a mechanic.

THE DEALERSHIP VS. COUSIN BILLY BOB'S GARAGE

Nearly every customer that comes into my shop says, "I have a (insert relative) that is a mechanic". I'll let him do that repair. I always probe that answer with a question. Where does he work? Or, what dealership is he at? I cringe when the answer is something like, "He works on elevators". Wow, I am sure he is a top-notch elevator mechanic. I am sure that the elevator companies train him well. I am also sure that you do not want my dealership mechanic working on the elevator at your favorite shopping center, apartment building or high-rise. My dealership mechanic, just like the elevator guy could probably figure it out - eventually. They really should stick to each one's expertise.

Everyone has a brother, cousin or friend who is a mechanic. Maybe even some of them have been to tech school or even have a certification. Where did that certification come from? I once saw on late night TV that I can get my mechanics certification mail order. I love certificates too. Now days anyone can go down the street to the copy shop, make a logo and print it out on very nice paper. Does that qualify them to install brakes on your Ford, Nissan or German car? I am not sure. Are you? Imagine the simple task of putting brakes on a car. Sounds pretty simple I am sure. Would you trust your cars BRAKES to a half baked mechanic? So why seek them out to install parts on the most complex and safety related components on one of your LARGEST INVESTIMENTS?

As a manager, consultant and auto dealership executive, I am biased. This is because I spend thousands and thousands of dollars each month and year to train my technicians to repair brake systems. Along with brakes, the other systems on your car are complex. Each and every system is intergraded with the main computer or electronic control unit. I don't want Cousin Bobbie or Joe the mechanic working on my Ford Focus Brakes. From the least expensive KIA or Hyundai to the most complex Audi or Porsche, BMW or Jaguar, those parts of a car are sophisticated. We need a trained mechanic fixing our cars.

Yes the independent shops have training. They are not manufacturer specific. They teach generalities. And they teach second and third hand. The manufacturer did not train most of the instructors. Most learned it by trial and ERROR. Those errors are on your cars. And I suspect you paid for it too.

Remember, you bought a car, and you have to take care of it! You cannot neglect your car just because it cannot speak to you!

3

MAINTAINING YOUR VEHICLE

It is very important to know how to maintain your vehicle and understand what and when to say yes to certain items on the car. I will take you thru a sample maintenance plan. We will start at five thousand miles and go up thru one hundred thousand miles.

SAMPLE MAINTENANCE PLAN

5,000-Mile Service. This can be called a Minor Service. It is typically an oil and filter change only. Many dealers will and should ask you if you would like a courtesy inspection. Always say yes. It's free! They will make sure your car is road worthy for your next trip or your daily drive. Rarely should you need anything additional at this mileage interval. **Let's call this the LOF and Inspection.** *LOF means lube oil and filter*

10,000-Mile Service. This is also a Minor Service. This 10k is typically an oil and filter change and possibly a tire rotation. The tire rotation depends upon your car. Some cars have different style wheels between the front and back. If this is the case, it's just an Oil and Filter change. Don't forget the courtesy inspection. Rarely again should you need anything. You should not have to pay for anything extra. **And again it's an LOF, Inspection, and possible tire rotation.**

15,000-Mile Service. This service could be an intermediate service. It is still oil and filter change, maybe an air filter or pollen filter. A courtesy inspection is still a good idea. There may be some light bulbs necessary. Usually these are under warranty. If not I bet the dealer will install them free of charge. **This would be LOF, Courtesy Inspection, possible Air Filter and Pollen Filter.**

20,000-Mile Service. This is just like the 10k Minor Service. **And again it's an LOF, Courtesy Inspection, and possible tire rotation.**

25,000-Mile Service. This is a regular 5k Minor Service. **Let's call this the LOF and Inspection.**

30,000-Mile Service. This becomes a Major Service. Everything gets looked over during a Major Service; they should go over the car, the engine and transmission with a fine toothcomb. The cost of this can range from the low $300's on up. I have seen them cost upwards of $1000. Some highline European cars cost much more. Be very leery of these very expensive ones. Always consult your owner's manual to compare what is recommended at this Major interval.

This is an area where you can get taken advantage. Most dealerships offer the manufacturer specific service. Ask if the service is exactly what is recommended in the owner's manual. PLEASE ASK.

TOP SECRET

Consult your owners' manual for the exact maintenance schedule for your car.

Stop! Go back and read that Top Secret again.

Now do it one more time.

A Sample Maintenance Checklist

MAINTENANCE MILEAGE 000S	5	10	15	20	25	30	45	60	90	120
SERVICES										
Oil and Filter	X	X	X	X	X	X	X	X	X	X
Courtesy Inspection	X	X	X	X	X	X	X	X	X	X
Air Filter (Check)	X	X	X	X	X	X	X	X	X	X
Pollen Filter (Check)	X	X	X	X	X	X	X	X	X	X
Wiper Blades (Check)	X	X	X	X	X	X	X	X	X	X
Light Bulbs (Check)	X	X	X	X	X	X	X	X	X	X
Brake Inspection	X	X	X	X	X	X	X	X	X	X
Nitrogen Service (FREE)	X	X	X	X	X	X	X	X	X	X
Fuel Filter Replace						X		X		
Transmission Fluid Exchange					X		X	X	X	

Coolant Fluid Exchange					X		X	X	X
Brake Fluid Exchange					X		X	X	X

Your owner's manual can save you money if you just read it. The manufacturers should make customers take a test on the owner's manual before you leave the dealership when you purchase a car. It is that important.

Recently, I had a customer call me about his car. He was angry too. He claimed we had the car in the shop three times and we cannot fix his dome light. He also claimed that one of my technicians even came out to the service drive and inspected the car with him on his last visit. He just could not understand how his car is still having the same problem. So naturally when I received the phone call I was empathetic to the situation and I asked some probing questions.

Question. What year, make and model car do you drive?

Answer. 2005 Porsche Cayenne

Question. When did the problem start?

Answer. Since I bought my vehicle

Question. How many miles on the car?

Answer. 32,000 Miles

What is happening to the car? What are the symptoms? I asked. He told that his dome light was not operating correctly. He told me the floor lights stayed on all the time. But if he hit the dome light switch repeatedly the light would go off. So I decided to employ my favorite technique. I responded to him that my foreman and I would head to his office and take a look. What could I do? He was at work and was having repeated problems. So we trekked a few miles to the office and his parking garage. My customer demonstrated his concern to us. After a thorough explanation of the concern from the customer, we decided to open the owner's manual and do some research. Yep there it was, on page 150 of the owner's manual. The proper operating instructions for the overhead lights and the floor mood lighting system were detailed right in front of us. After a bit of embarrassment by the customer that we shrugged off, we all laughed. I made a customer for life. He bought both of us an ice cream bar for our troubles.

Moral. Always read your owners manual. You will save years of frustration.

It's interesting to me how as I write the book these scenarios keep appearing in real life. Back to maintenance!

Now there is nothing wrong with some additional services at this mileage interval. The key is to compare with your owners manual and make sure you have full disclosure on the additional services being performed. Always ask for a detailed explanation of the additional services.

Just remember at 30,000 miles; **let's just call this an expensive service.**

Many California dealerships got into serious trouble by not disclosing the difference between what the manufacturer recommends and what the dealership recommends.

Here is the difference. The manufacturer engineers need to keep the cost down as a sales tool for the product. The manufacturer recommends the minimum specification to keep your car running. I liken it to exercise for your body. We should drink a certain amount of water; take the recommended amount of vitamins, and exercise just right each day. The minimum is what we need. Sometimes a little bit more is better.

Each and every customer drives differently. Other factors that contribute to your maintenance and repair needs are road conditions or highway speeds. Local traffic makes a difference. Also, do you gun it from the stoplight? There are many variables in your maintenance. One such example is stop and go traffic. Constant stopping and starting puts more wear on your car than normal highway driving. Southern California, specifically Los Angeles area drivers' area drivers should usually follow the extreme maintenance plan for their cars. Everyone has heard of the 405 Freeway. Just try to get thru the 405 – 10 interchange during rush hour. Besides the headache tension on bodies, just imagine the quick starts and stops. Accelerate! Now brake! Now accelerate again, wait brake! This is wear and tear on your drive train and brakes. It's stop-and-go 24 hours a day. Rush hour in Los Angeles can take years off your vehicle. Just follow the manufactures guidelines and you will be fine.

It also depends on the purpose of your car. Did you lease the car and plan on turning it in at 36,000 miles. Or are you going to keep the car for a long period of time. Only a trained technician can tell you what is needed at that point in the life of the car.

I propose having the service advisor do the minimum recommended by the manufacturer. During the service have the courtesy inspection performed by the technician. Then finally discuss the recommended services with you at a convenient time. This should keep your car in great shape!

35,000 & 40,000 Mile Services. These are typically a minor service. **Let's call these the LOF and Inspection.**

45,000-Mile Service. This service could be an intermediate service as well. Still an oil and filter change, maybe an air filter or pollen filter. A courtesy inspection is still a good idea. There may be some light bulbs necessary. They may look at the fuel filter. Depending on the Manufacturer of the car, and the warranty terms, the car may be out of warranty. **This would be LOF, Courtesy Inspection, possible Air Filter and Pollen Filter.**

60,000-Mile Service. This becomes a Major Service again. Remember everything gets looked over during a Major Service; they should go over the car including the engine and transmission with a fine toothcomb. The cost of this can range from the low $300's on up. I have seen them cost upwards of $1000. Be very leery of these very expensive ones. Always consult your owner's manual to compare what is recommended at this Major interval.

Again, this is an interval where someone could try to take advantage of you. *Well previously, because you are reading this book, that will not happen.* Most dealerships offer the manufacturer specific service. Ask if the service is exactly what is recommended in the owner's manual. PLEASE ASK.

You may have noticed that the schedule starts repeating itself after 30,000 miles. Most manufacturers do this. There of course is the odd exception. At 60,000 miles, **this again is an expensive service.** The services repeat at 90,000, 120,000 and so on.

OTHER MAINTENANCE ITEMS

In addition to all of the regular service items, here is a guide to other service operations that you could need with a detailed description of what they are and about how much they should cost. Make sure to pay close attention to the warnings to if you do not stay on top of these items!

Coolant Service – The purposes of this procedure is for the mechanic to remove the old or contaminated fluid from the cooling system and replace it with fresh new fluid. This service is commonly called a coolant fluid exchange or coolant flush. A coolant service typically means that the mechanic drains the radiator and replaces about one gallon of coolant. A coolant fluid exchange is the replacement of the entire amount of coolant in the cooling system. If someone suggests to you that you need this service please ask for a thorough explanation.

Many manufactures claim to have lifetime coolant. Although coolant is supposed to last a lifetime in the engine, the system can become corroded and contaminated with the metallic parts of an engine and its cooling system components. In order to keep this from becoming too technical, I am ok with a service person recommending this service at the two-year or 30,000 mile mark. This again is suggested at the corresponding intervals, 30k, 60k, 90k, 120k…etc.

Brake System Service – The purpose of this procedure is for the mechanic to remove all of the brake fluid from the brake system components and brake lines and replace it with fresh new fluid. Sounds familiar? Over time the fluid in the brake system becomes hot and sometimes overheats. Once the heat dissipates, small particles of fluid remain mixed with the brake fluid. This lowers the boiling point of the fluid and could create a spongy brake pedal feeling.

Some will say to have your brake system bled. When you bleed the brakes, you typically only remove some of the fluid. The idea of the brake fluid exchange is to remove all of the contaminated fluid with fresh fluid.

I am ok with a service person recommending this service at the two-year or 30,000 mile mark. This again is suggested at the corresponding intervals, 30k, 60k, 90k, 120k…etc. Always ask the service person for a detailed explanation of the service they are performing. Many dealerships have machines to monitor the brake fluid exchange, similar to a blood transfusion. The machines are programmed to verify the correct bleeding sequence is followed for removal of the fluid and the correct amount of new fluid is replaced.

Transmission Service –Most transmissions hold anywhere from 5 – 12 quarts of transmission fluid. Some even have more fluid. The purpose of a transmission service is to remove the contaminated fluid along with the metallic shavings and automatic clutch material or debris. I feel like I may be repeating myself here. Most regular services only allow the mechanic to drain about 4 quarts of transmission fluid. If the dealership offers a complete fluid exchange, this is the better service to have performed. During a transmission fluid exchange all the fluid is pumped out and new fluid is pumped into the transmission. Typically new vehicles do not require a filter. The complete fluid exchange does the trick.

Warning: if you have not been maintaining your transmission throughout the life of the vehicle, beware of having this service performed at higher mileages. I suggest not performing this service after 75,000 miles if you have not been maintaining your transmission. This service could lead to more problems down the road if not immediately.

Fuel Injection Service - This is a complicated issue so I sought the advice of a fuel system expert. And to make this very easy to understand I will explain it this way. Our engines are more complicated and running hotter these days to achieve a higher efficiency and greater fuel economy. The government requires the gasoline refineries to add chemical additives in their fuel to meet EPA standards. This heat combined with poor fuel causes build up on the fuel injectors themselves and the engine valves. Over time, in some cases, one-year or around 15,000 miles the engine could develop a loss of performance.

I was the lucky driver of a 2006 Hummer H2. At about 13,500 miles my truck began to experience a rough idle and a lower performance. So what did I do? I took it to the Hummer Dealer in Torrance, California. They recommended a complete fuel system service. Even though I knew the answer, I asked for an explanation and also asked if Hummer would pay for this service. The advisor gave me a good talk about fuel and then politely told me that this is not a warrantable item. He was right. There was no manufacturer defect in my engine; it was just a buildup of carbon and deposits. I approved the repair. Then I asked for a discount. Guess what. My service, which was supposed to cost $150, was performed for $100 bucks.

The important thing here is to understand that this is real and can happen to your car. The simple thing to do is have a technician look at the car and determine what is gummed up and have that system cleaned. If you want the extra protection have them install an additive to your gas tank too. It works.

Warning: Do not let someone tell you that this will **_greatly_** increase your fuel economy. There definately are benefits to the service, however if a service person says he/she can increase your fuel mileage, it's just not true. This guy is just selling you something. If you are having fuel economy issues, this service may help. Check your air filter too. Have the dealership check the computer system as well.

At anytime over 15,000 miles that you experience performance issues, this service could be performed to remedy the problem. It is not a cure all. Always ask for an explanation from the service advisor or manager.

Nitrogen Service - There is a lot of hullabaloo about nitrogen for your tires. Does it work — Yes! The real controversy is how much does it work. If you drive a NASCAR this is the service for you. Or if you have a fleet of autos or trucks, this service is for you.

Nitrogen molecules are larger than regular oxygen molecules, which help the air in your tires remain constant pressure. This in turn reduces wear on tires. The consistent air pressure along with the reduction in irregular tire wear helps with an increase in fuel economy. The actual amount of increase is minimal. I suggest that the increase is less than .1 of a mile per gallon. I have not seen any data to support my claim. It's just my humble opinion. It definitely will not hurt and you can claim to be GREEN with your nitrogen. If the place is really cool you can get some green valve stem caps to show off to you Hollywood friends. Most experts suggest that just keeping your tires properly filled will have about the same effect on fuel mileage and tire wear. Once during the 2008 Presidential Campaign, then Candidate Obama, talked about the importance of tire pressure and fuel mileage. Although the media ridiculed him, he was CORRECT!

On the other hand if you own a fleet of trucks or cars, nitrogen may just be the ticket for you. .1 mile per gallon adds up over time and multiple cars and thousands of tire life improvement.

I have a friend who owns a Toyota Prius. Each time he visits my dealership he asks for a refill of Nitrogen. He claims his car rides better with the hot juice.

NITROGEN TEST

If you have a tire pressure monitoring system (TPMS) in your vehicle you can actually see a difference with Nitrogen.

With regular air in your tires perform this test. On a cold morning check the TPMS, more than likely the tire pressure in all four tires will be different. As you drive and your tires warm up, most of the time the tire pressure will even out. Once the car is warm the tire pressure will remain constant throughout the rest of the day.

On a vehicle with Nitrogen you will notice all the tires will have the same pressure from start up cold to warm. Or possibly the tires will all start out the same pressure and rise at the same rate as well. If you just want to be green – go for it. If you want real results – make you service advisor check the air in your tires every time you come in for service.

Now that you know what a maintenance plan should look like per miles, and what the services are, it is important to get your car a regular check-up! MANY TIMES THESE ARE FREE!!!! Most dealerships will offer a courtesy inspection. Always say yes to the inspection. In fact, always ask for it when you take your car in for any service.

TIRES

Tires are arguably the most important safety item on your car. Tire maintenance is critical to performance, fuel economy and safety. Most auto manufacturers recommend you rotate your tires every 5,000 – 10,000 miles. Each vehicle has a different mileage or time period for maintenance. I would recommend that you keep your tires inflated to the proper level. This easy check can be performed by you or your dealership in a matter of seconds. This should be looked at monthly or at least done every time you have your oil and filter change. Naturally the service department will do this for you at no charge.

Many dealerships are working hard to be your full service provider. This means they want to take care of your repairs and maintenance including tires. Most dealership service departments have access directly to the tire manufacturer or one of its representatives.

There is a well known statistic that shows; the first person who recommends tires to a customer is usually the person who sells the tires to a customer. The dealership is competitive on tires. The actual profit margin on a tire sale is considerably lower that other repairs.

If the profit margin is low in tire sales, does it make you wonder why everyone wants to sell you tires? The reason is because tires are the key to the rest of your car as well. Once an auto repair shop removes your tires, they have been given the approval to inspect the rest of the steering and suspension components on your car. Under the wrong circumstances this can be detrimental to your wallet.

Again, this is a critical reason why you should understand the questions to ask your dealership. You should absolutely want the service technician to report any safety condition to you. You want to have your cheat sheet to ask the questions about the necessity of the repairs.

When you are ready to purchase tires, contact the dealership and inquire about tire sales. Many dealerships stock tires. They can usually do this for you immediately.

COURTESY INSPECTIONS

What is a courtesy inspection? A courtesy inspection is another name for an inspection of your car. Many dealerships call this a 21-point inspection. Some have 27 points and others have 100-point inspections. The purpose of the inspection points is to have a technician look your car over to ensure all of the components are in working order for your driving needs. Please, do not ever pay some dealership to look over your car. Dealerships should do this free of charge every time.

TOP SECRET

**Ask for a World Class Inspection™
every time your car is in the shop.**

The reason a dealership would do this is for 1) customer satisfaction and 2) the ability to sell you additional work that needs to be performed 3) to develop a trusting relationship. Regardless of the reason it is done; ask for this every time your car is in the shop.

The reason is simple. You want to be informed as to what is going on with your car. And you want to be partners with the repairing dealership. Remember this. If they look your car over and it looks great, you have peace of mind. You also have a commitment from the dealership that your car is safe and sound. The wheels are not going to fall off and the wiper blades will keep your windshield clean for the next period of time until you are lucky enough to see the dealership again. Also, you want to determine if you can trust your dealership. If they try to sell you something early on in the ownership of the vehicle, I suggest you tread lightly.

If you come in to the dealership for the first couple or three times and everything looks great, well, they are probably trustworthy. (Let's call this the courtesy inspection test.) If only at the higher mileage the car starts to need a few things, I say it's a good chance they are telling the truth.

I will say if you regularly service your car at the dealership, they will provide you with adequate information on your cars health. Most stores will own up to a misdiagnosis or something that they overlooked during an inspection.

If something fails and on the inspection report it is checked OK; sounds like leverage to me! That does not mean that the repair is going to be free. However, you have leverage to negotiate a deal.

I have had a time in my own shop where the mechanic performed the courtesy inspection. The mechanic said that everything was great, including the brakes. Guess what: the brakes wore out before the next service. The backing plates on the pads ground right into the rotors. Well my customer rightfully so, explained her situation and showed me her report. She received FREE rotors from my store. I politely fixed the error in her favor. I asked her to pay for the brake pads and we paid for the extra work done. This was a great deal for the customer. She saved $100's.

If my mechanic had caught this during an inspection, she would have paid for the brake pads then and possibly the rotors too. However, she got a break on my goof.

Once at my Audi store, a customer came in for a recall. The recall stated to check the belt for wear. It only said check the belt. Audi paid for the technician to check the belt. The belt looked great and there was no problem. Guess what! The belt tensioner was bad. Now no one said to look at this part, however we told the customer everything was ok. He could keep going and not to worry. A few days later the engine blew up. To make a long story shorter, the customer paid about $1200 for a NEW engine. It cost my store nearly $5000. The simple reason is, we looked the car over and failed to notify him of the problem conditions. I could have been a hardnosed person and sent him down the road. However with the circumstances being what they were, I figured we had some responsibility and a court would most likely decide in his favor. He wins. The customer received a new engine.

Now on the flip side, when a dealership repair shop recommends something to you, they are most likely telling the truth. And if you decline the repair at this time, you are holding yourself liable for the repairs and the future damage to the car and its components.

In the same scenario as mentioned above: I have had numerous customers come into the store and have recommendations made to them. They declined. Guess what. The parts fail as suggested they would. If we recommend to you to have your brakes fixed, you better do it. Any future damage to your rotors is your baby. You own it. You are paying top dollar. I hate to say it, but *I told you so* is hard to swallow from your service advisor. It's worse than your husband or wife saying I told you so. This one comes with a price tag - usually a hefty one.

Each and every time you take your car in the shop you should have a courtesy inspection completed on the vehicle. While researching dealership performance, I have found a new and improved technique. This technique or procedure is called a "World Class Inspection™".

A world class inspection is a unique system that enables the service advisors and technicians to accurately find and present legitimately needed work to you in a consistent and professional manner. As a customer you will receive a full color report that spells out the details of your car. This report is called a "Know Your Vehicle Report™" or KYV. This KYV report will include a list of every item that the service advisor and technician looked at on your car. It also includes pictures and an explanation of the services needed. Most dealerships will also report back to you any items recommended by the manufacturer.

A world class inspection system works like this: The dealership invests time and training into its service advisors and technicians to teach them how to inspect your car. The dealership is teaching and training its technicians to inspect your car to give you peace of mind. They want you to know everything about your car and become educated on the needed maintenance and repair. This is the level of awareness you want regarding the requirements of your car. Now you will have the full picture. You as the customer will be in full control of what needs to be maintained or repaired.

The service advisors have been trained to be highly effective and comfortable presenting the Know Your Vehicle™ report. This report highlights the recommended services and costs in an informative manner that is easy to read and comprehend. As a customer, you will come to expect the Know Your Vehicle™ report as part of the service experience.

Imagine if your service advisor gave you a 7 – 11 page full color report with the items on your car prioritized from most important to least important. The items are color coded in a very simple and easy to understand method.

It is color coded RED — YELLOW — GREEN.

- **Items denoted in Red — this item needs attention immediately.**

- **Items denoted in Yellow — this item will require attention in the future.**

- **Items denoted in Green — this item is OK!**

Now you can decide what to fix and what to wait on. You are in total control. You can make the decision at home with your spouse and budget your auto repair without the pressure of the service person expecting an answer. This service is only offered in a new car dealership.

I suggest when your dealership service advisor asks you if you would like a courtesy inspection completed on your car; you tell them YES and "Make it World Class".

Finally, tell them to do it for **FREE!**

With all this being said, let's discuss **WHEN** to believe your service consultant and what to buy

With all this being said, let's discuss **WHEN** to believe your service consultant and what to buy

WHAT TO ASK YOUR SERVICE CONSULTANT

When a service consultant asks you if you would like your vehicle inspected, say, "YES. Absolutely, please call me at a convenient time and review the findings."

Here are the questions to ask.

- *What is the total cost of the repair? Please itemize the labor and the parts prices.*

- You are entitled to a breakdown of the parts and labor for the repair. The service person should be able to confidently break down the prices and give you a quote. If he stammers and says, "UH well UH, UH I'm not sure." Or anything like that. RUN. Politely say thank you and ask for the time your car will be completed. He is not trained correctly and could be trying to take advantage of you.

- *What is your labor rate? How many flat rate labor hours are your charging?*

- According to most authorities, repair facilities do not have to post their actual labor rate. However if a repair facility does post the rate, they are supposed to charge that rate or less if they choose. The fun part comes in when repair shops do not post their actual rate. The dealership can charge your anything they want per hour. Most have an hourly rate; let's use $100 per hour.

It's about reasonable, depending on when you are reading this. In a few years someone is going to say, "I remember the good ole days when labor was only $100 per hour". In San Francisco some dealerships AND independent shops are getting $200 per hour.

For this story let's use $100 per hour. You can calculate it easily. The fun comes in when a dealership uses a Matrix or pricing grid or price escalator to determine the labor rate. A price matrix or escalator adjusts the labor rate based on many different criteria. Most of the time, the labor rate adjustment is going UP. Because most service advisors do not know how to respond to this when asked by a customer. YOU WIN AGAIN! It is legal and acceptable to charge on a pricing escalator or pricing grid. You as a consumer though need to know how you are being charged. If the shop is using one correctly, the service person should tell you that they charge each repair by the job. And they do not have a labor rate per hour.

This is similar to an oil and filter change. When you get your oil changed, do you care how much the parts and labor is separately. Mostly, you want it done for the best price. Example $19.95. Who cares that the parts are usually 17.00 and the labor is 2.95, right. What is the hourly rate? It works out to about 12.00

per hour. Less than most technicians make. It is a loser for the dealership, but it really does not matter to you. And it should not.

Dealers like any other business have a cost structure. They need to maintain a certain rate per hour of labor charged. And you are going to pay it one way or the other. I discount my services for those common maintenance items. I have to make up for it in other areas. And those areas are the highly skilled areas of the car. Electronics are in every part of the car now. Vehicles are more sophisticated than almost any other item you own. A vehicle computer is more sophisticated than your home pc. But you will spend hundreds of dollars on computer repair. Or you will toss it out and buy a new one. Unfortunately the cost of vehicle computer repair is much higher than home pc work. I have friends who charge over $100 per hour to work on my network at the office. My network is not nearly as sophisticated as your car. Yet we gladly spend money for anything but our cars.

So when a dealership tells you the price for a component to be fixed, he should confidently be able to explain how he derived the price. If not, ask a few questions.

On a major repair, you have to decide if the $money$ the dealership is charging is acceptable to your pocket book. If it is, then have the work done. If it is more than you can afford or want to afford, then politely decline the repair for a moment. You may still choose to have the work done, just not quite yet.

We still need more information.

- **What is the component that they are repairing or servicing?**

  Your service advisor should be able to explain to you exactly what they are fixing. Ask for a thorough explanation of the part that they are repairing.

- **Has the part failed? Or is this for maintenance only?**

  It is important to know why you are replacing the parts. If the part has failed then it becomes a priority to have repaired. If it is going to cause additional damage to the car, the priority level just increased again. If the part is just being done for maintenance, you have some options. Ask the next question.

- **How long will these parts last?**

  Find out how long the parts will last if the parts are not fixed immediately. Ask if will cause other problems if not fixed today.

- **What is the most important item that needs to be fixed today?**

  Many times multiple items need to be fixed. Ask your service advisor to rank the items in order of importance. What really needs to be done now? What can wait? The service advisor should give you this information. Also ask him to remind you with a phone call when you should have the rest of the repairs completed.

- ***Can I have a discount?***

    Always ask for a price reduction! We are car dealers, let's make a deal with you. I am not sure that you will get one, but come on: ASK! A good reputable dealership will have trained his people to answer these questions. All dealerships are different when it comes to their expense structure. The key is to get the best deal for you. And if they decline the discount, it is because they are fully trained and have answered your questions correctly and completely. And I submit that they are a busy well-run organization.

This is not to say that well-run stores do not offer price concessions. I ran a very highline European dealership. I made deals every day. There are many different reasons for this. I especially worked with my customers on items that we called defection points.

A defection point by definition is: a point in the lifecycle of the vehicle where a customer can "defect" or leave the dealership and go to an independent shop.

This is on items like, tires, brakes, batteries and alignments. Typically a consumer has the option, or thinks that an independent shop can perform these minor repairs at a cheaper price than the dealership. Consumers driven shops will price themselves in line to be competitive with the after-market places.

Japanese automakers have always been maintenance driven companies. Ask any owner of a Japanese car about maintenance. Most are committed to keeping their cars on the road. Many times Japanese vehicle owners are even more knowledgeable of their vehicle than the domestic vehicle owners.

The Ford Motor Company took the lead in the domestic world with this new philosophy. This began in the late 1990's. Ford Motor Company has been a driver of domestic dealerships getting into the business of taking care of customers. As the business has evolved, and especially in today's market, cars don't break like they did before. Consumers are becoming more maintenance savvy. Dealerships are beginning to understand the importance of being competitive on certain items, especially those that are defection points.

And I ask you to get your tires at the dealership. Get your alignment done at the dealership too. Those men and women really understand how your car works. However, make sure you only pay a reasonable price. It is always good to do your homework on tire prices. Many dealerships offer price matching or price beating. I even think you can get free tire rotations for life with the purchase of a set of tires. You can probably get a free alignment with a set of tires. The bargains are out there.

Many consumers, like yourself have already compared the competition or heard one of the zillion commercials on television, radio or the Internet telling you how cheap you can have your car fixed. Heck, I heard an ad recently giving away professional basketball tickets to have an oil change. Imagine how much you will spend once you are there to get those free babies.

THE MOST IMPORTANT
ADVICE I CAN OFFER

If you only read one section of this book, here is the one specifically. When the service advisor presents you with your vehicle service needs, the needs should be presented to you in this order.

- **Safety Items**

- **Primary Concern**

- **Failed Items on your car**

- **Maintenance Items**

- **Other or Other Caution Items**

Let me explain. You might ask why the service advisor should present the safety items to me before my primary concern. When you bring your vehicle into the shop and they perform the complimentary vehicle inspection, the initial thought is to have them tell you what is wrong with your car. Have the dealer tell you how much it is going to cost to fix what you brought it in for, right? One thing you want the dealer to do is examine your car and ensure your safety.

For example: you show up at the dealership with a check engine light flashing on the dash board, the dealership diagnoses the car and determines that a sensor is out of parameters. Great. They give you the estimate and you give the approval. Again great! Ops, your rear tire has the metal cord sticking out. The tire could blow out any minute. It sounds extreme but it does happen. If you have the choice to fix a flashing light because of a sensor that is out of parameters or fix a tire that might blow out. It is your choice. My thought is to fix the rear tire first. Then if time and money permit, fix the light second.

Now you have a clear choice of what the priority is on your car. The dealership is the expert on auto repair. Let them, make them or demand that they accept the responsibility to keep you informed of your needs.

After the repairs are prioritized you can schedule how you want to have them completed. The next items to be looked at are the items that have failed. This way you know the severity. It is more important to correct a failed item than routine maintenance. Next review the maintenance items such as an oil service or the ones listed above for completion. Finally, after all of those are complete, then go ahead and take care of the OTHER items such as the cosmetic items, or comfort items.

Ultimately you should take care of your car the way you want to take care of it. I am sure that I will take care of mine differently than you. When my car is in for service, I want to know the good and the bad so I am an informed decision maker. Using these rules or guidelines will make you informed as well. Your pocket book will thank you.

Now and only now, you can make an educated decision. You are well armed with the information you need to decide whether to spend your hard earned dollars on this car.

There are so many items that can be inspected and reviewed to be replaced, I could list them in a catalog size book and never list them all. It does boil down to trust of the dealership. And especially trust of the service advisor or consultant working with you and your car. When we start a new relationship with a boy or a girl, we asked a lot of questions. As we begin to trust them, we take their word for it. So it is important to know these lucky 7 questions when going in for the first few times - or before you reach for your wallet.

And after all that, if you feel insecure, ask for the manager. That is his job. He is in the position to oversee the department. And he or she is there to be your advocate as well. Most managers want to build a good relationship with the community. Most will have your best interest at heart. But as one famous president said "trust, but verify."

I have just listed seven questions that can make you more informed. These questions will also help you avoid being ripped off. After asking one or all of these you should feel confident to either having the work performed or politely declining the repairs.

SERVICES TO AVOID

What is a Johnson Valve? I don't know! Do not buy it.

Should you change the air in your tires? Air does not go bad! Think about it. I worked at a Ferrari Dealership; we would joke about the Italian Air in the tires. It makes the car faster.

Muffler Bearings…. NOT. If they tell you that you have one, make them show it to you. I heard something about a Chrysler muffler bearing once. Don't buy it!

Seriously there are some services that you should be leery of purchasing.

Engine Flush. They make machines that flush your engine oil and supposedly clean your engine block. I recommend avoiding that service. Sometimes it can cause more damage to the engine than it prevents.

Shocks. Please stop buying shocks! If a shock fails, normally it is leaking oil. I suggest shocks will last you 100,000 miles or more. If you are due for shocks, your car needs a lot more than just shocks. I have been working at the dealership for over 20 years. I can count on one hand how many shocks that I have replaced. What is ridiculous is that the shock industry is a multimillion-dollar industry. I say it is not necessary most of the time it is offered. The shock makers have created a market for themselves. They have created and won the PR battle when it comes to shock replacement.

The other night I was driving down the 10 Freeway in Los Angeles with my girlfriend. She noticed this 1970s model Cadillac convertible driving in the lane next to us. The car was floating all over the road and bouncing from lane to lane and the families inside we having a wonderful time. She stated to me, "I think they need shocks". I politely responded, honey they need springs first. Shocks will assist the springs from expanding and collapsing but they cannot stop a worn out suspension system from bouncing. The point is shocks may fix a symptom however the shocks will be worn out again shortly if the problem is not repaired first.

Here is the one question to ask about shocks. Ask the man "are my tires cupped"? If he says yes, go touch the

tires yourself. **The tires will feel wavy as you move your hand around them.**

I am sure that Caddy's tires were cupped. Rarely will this happen to your vehicle. Call me when your car is thirty years old. Then we can talk shocks.

When someone tries to sell you something that you are not sure of, just ask those questions. Find out the manufacturers recommended replacement interval. Ask another expert or call the service manager at the dealership.

WHAT TO DO WITH DEALERSHIP COUPON OFFERS

My mom who does work a full time job is a coupon clipper for her car. I don't think she has paid for an oil change for three years. She waits for those big ole dealership mailers to show up at the door, and then she heads out to get a free oil change or tire rotation. She would ask me questions about the dealership or what she should do.

My answer.

Say NO to everything. Get IN and Get OUT right away!!!

It was not because I thought she was going to get ripped off, but because I thought she would buy what they were selling. I am sure she needed the work done, but I only wanted her to have the maintenance done at one location. If they gave her a report, I would make her take it to the dealership down the street from our house. I liked them best and I had a solid relationship with them. And of course I wanted to patronize my community dealership.

Just recently, a dealership in our town was having a fifteenth anniversary sale. Free Oil change and tire rotation. My mom did not even need her oil changed. She went anyway. Those deals are out there. If all you want is a bargain, just do as my mother does, wait, or read the newspaper and find some great deals out there.

Many times dealers will honor other dealers and some independent shop prices. Grab your best coupon from the newspaper and drive into the dealership. How much will you bet me that the dealership will do the same repair for the same price as the independent shop? Talk about a loyalty builder. These guys want your business.

I goofed as a manager once and ran an advertisement that read, Free Minor Service and we would do it in 30 minutes or the next ones free, too. Gees imagine the response. Good thing my store was prepared to handle quick maintenance. I did the maintenance in 30 minutes and had enough time left over to inspect the car and make some recommendations as well.

Understand one thing with a mail piece. This piece is designed to get you in the dealership. Ok, that's advertising. Remember there is no such thing as a free lunch. If I advertise that my oil change is cheap or free today, my goal is to let you know about other things on your car. I want to sell you the regular higher priced items.

I have spent a lifetime perfecting advertising for dealerships. And let me tell you, I am good at getting you in the door for service. Let me tell you we dealer people can be very enticing when we want to. I partnered with an advertising agency recently. My dealership offered Free Inspections to our customers, - One Day Only. I generated over $100,000 from that mail piece. Dealership advertising works. I want you to realize why you are getting the great deal. It is simply to sell you more things. Just be cautious and ask lots of questions. If you can get through all of the questions I laid out earlier and you feel comfortable, and then authorize the work. Do not forget to ask for a deal.

KEEP YOUR RECORDS

Many dealerships compete for your business and send out discount coupons, which lure you away. That comes with responsibility on both parts. If you are unhappy with your current dealership and decide to switch to another, KEEP YOUR RECORDS.

My best friend has a Volvo station wagon. Her husband was actually a mechanic at a dealership (of a different make). He would take their car in and do the services on the car when it was necessary. And he always bought cheap parts at the auto parts store. He never kept a record of any of his maintenance oil changes and so on.

Well, one day the turbo-charger went out. When she drove the car into the Volvo shop for repairs, the dealership told her what had happened and that she needed a new turbo charger unit. The cost was around $3000. She stated, "I had a Volvo extended service contract on the car." Guess what! They denied her repairs from her extended warranty. For the simple reason, she could not produce any maintenance records. They were extremely nice and courteous; however they flat out denied the repair under extended warranty contract.

She then called me and asked for help. As a good friend I made some calls tried to pull a few strings. I even called a friend who was a Volvo service manager. I was able to get a discount on the repair, but I could not get the repair covered under her contract. She had no documentation period! The manufacturer, which was Volvo, did a great job with me as far as communication but they were inflexible and stated that without documentation of maintenance services the warranty was void. $2000 later she had a new turbo. Still she spent $2000 when it could have been covered for free.

And that brings up the issue of warranties...

4

EXTENDED WARRAITY PURCHASES

Extended warranties are insurance policies sold to protect your car against breakdown in the future. They typically start when your vehicle leaves the manufacturer's warranty period. Many have additional features like rental coverage, towing and some even allow for travel benefits if you car breaks down outside of your hometown.

Each manufacturer sells an extended warranty for your car. These are their insurance policies to cover your car in the event of a break down. Like any insurance policy, the person who is selling this warranty is gambling that your car will not break down. And they are gambling that they will make money on your money.

Extended warranties can be lumped into two categories.

- **The ones backed by the Auto Manufacturer**
- **The ones that are <u>NOT</u> backed by the Auto Manufacturer**

In the case of a manufacturer warranty, the Auto Manufacturer backs up this warranty. You are gambling that your car may break down in the future. You are putting up your money now so that you will not have a greater expense in a few years. This manufacturer-based warranty is the only warranty that I advocate you should purchase.

Usually there are different levels of coverage from basic coverage to some sort of premium coverage. I always suggest the premium coverage. This is a close to the original manufacturer's warranty as you can buy. When affordable, buy it! The other warranties are good they only cover fewer components. Most customers hear the words bumper-to-bumper warranty. The premium warranty does not cover quite that much but close. Some manufacturer warranties cover power train components. This is good for covering the Engine, Transmission and Power train components. How would you like to spend $1000-$1500 for a warranty and only to find later that it just covers the internal engine components? Or to find that the fuel injector is not covered. When your car breaks down many years later after the original warranty has expired, this is not the time to discover that certain parts are not covered.

Premium Coverage Extended Warranties usually cover every part on the car that is included in the original warranty except maintenance items like tires, spark plugs, and paints or trim items.

Power Train Coverage Extended Warranties usually cover the internal engine, internal transmission and drive train parts. This means that they do cover an engine failure.

They would replace a piston or connecting rod in the engine. They will cover hydraulically lubricated parts in an engine or transmission. Automatic transmissions have hydraulic clutches inside them. These parts are typically covered under the manufacturer extended warranty. The rest of the power train or drive train is usually a component. These parts include the drive shaft and the differential gears. The differential gears make the turning motion of the engine turn the car forward.

Shortly we will talk about getting assistance with your car outside the warranty period. The auto manufacturers look to determine if you purchased a warranty. This is a great tool to show that you did your part in keeping your car maintained.

The manufacturer warranties will say the name of the manufacturer in the title. An example would be Ford Extended Service Plan or Ford ESP. Do not be fooled by other warranties that do not say the name of the manufacturer. You could be getting ripped off.

Many new car dealerships and used car dealerships sell other brands of warranties. Did you ever get a call about two years into your ownership of your car and the person on the phone was trying to sell you a warranty for your car? Hang up immediately. Most of these are selling aftermarket products. There are so many different versions on the market of these types of bogus, useless warranties. Who is backing up the plan? Even though it is possible that a reputable firm might back the plan TODAY, what about tomorrow?

Let's say you finance your car through your local credit union. And the loan officer recommends that you purchase an extended warranty. Do it. Just do it at the dealership. What does your credit union loan officer know about cars? What does he care in a few years when you break down? Insurance policies are lucrative. Everyone makes money selling them. Your loan office more than likely does not know about the turbo charger on your new Porsche. Or how does he know about the special exhaust system on your new Chevrolet Corvette? How does he know if those parts are covered components? Your manufacturer warranty is much more likely to cover these specialty items.

TOP SECRET

Your credit union loan officer does not care about your car.

The aftermarket guys and the credit unions have very little knowledge about what is needed when you are in a pinch. Who is going to cover your rental car? Will they? What happens during a parts delay?

Take this example. Let's say you have a Hyundai and it breaks down. You need an alternator to be replaced. It is a simple everyday part. Opps! The part is on back order. Your aftermarket warranty pays for five days of rental car. Now you are entering the second week waiting for the part. What do you do? Call Hyundai maybe? First question the service rep will ask you is, "Do you have an extended warranty?" And of course you answer yes. I bought it from Mr. Jones down at the bank. Guess what the next response is going to be…

If you had a Hyundai Warranty, the leverage you have is tremendous. You have THEIR product; THEIR warranty and you are waiting on THEIR parts. What do you think you will get? I would bet a free rental car. Then I would ask to waive the deductible for the warranty too. You just may get that too!

I have seen quite a few people come to my service departments with a problem. They flash their warranty contract and expect it to be covered. This is only to find the warranty company has gone out of business. Now what? You are done. Most of the time there is no recourse. Who will refund the money? What money? Oh yeah there are laws and such. Who has time to go thru all of that and hope that maybe you get some of your money back. The problem is your car is still broken and you need it fixed.

Let's just suppose that they are in business. The dealership calls the service line for the warranty company. Remember the warranty company is an insurance policy. Have you ever heard of insurance companies declining coverage? That is their job. Save the policy money for the insurance company. It happens more than I care to share with you. Time after time I have seen insurance companies decline coverage. We as a dealer usually get blamed for this problem.

Let's be clear on a couple things. As a new car dealership, we perform warranty repairs for the manufacturer. The manufacturer pays us. The manufacturer usually sends a check or credits the dealership bank account each month for the warranty repairs that it makes.

This simply means if the dealership makes a repair, the auto manufacturer will pay the dealership for it. If it is a manufacturer-based warranty, the manufacturer pays that as well. There are those rare times when the manufacturer denies a claim. This is usually when a consumer does not take care of the proper maintenance of the car. In my story of my friend and her Volvo, she did not have the proper maintenance records to show she changed the oil in her engine.

In the other scenario, we are both at the mercy of the big bad insurance company. They make the rules and we both just play the game. Where there is a conflict you are typically dealing with a representative that does not have your best interest at heart. A manufacturer-based warranty always worries about the consumer repurchase option. They want your repeat purchase and sometimes can be more flexible.

With your aftermarket warranty, I say it's a crapshoot. As a service advisor myself, I have called aftermarket companies and some have been great. Sometimes you just never know. Of course you are sent a policy with all the items that they cover. But what about that new widget that's on your hot rod; is it covered?

Another option is that some new car dealers sell their own extended warranty that is covered by the dealerships money. This is a decent alternative, but not as effective as the manufacturer's warranty. Sometimes, however, the price is much better on these warranties. BUT, remember, you get what you pay for. I suggest you stay with the real deal and only purchase the manufacturer warranty.

A WELL TIME EXAMPLE

Today at my dealership a customer came in with a problem. He was driving an Audi A8. For those of you that do not know what this is, well it is an expensive Audi.

When purchased new, the car can cost around $100,000. He actually bought his used, from a BMW dealership. Although I can forgive him this sin, what happened next is exactly what I want you to avoid. Let's call him Sully Smith. Upon purchasing his $100,000 vehicle from another make of dealership, Mr. Smith wanted to do the right thing and purchase an extended warranty.

Sounds right?

Well, he purchased this warranty for about $4500.

It must be a good warranty?

Must be good because he bought it from a dealership?

Right?

Not necessarily. THE PROBLEM? He needed some engine work and it was covered by the extended warranty. However, the warranty company did not want to pay my rates, they only wanted to pay a discounted amount of labor time. The repair total was $5000. The extended warranty company only wanted to pay $3700 bucks.

Who is going to get stuck with the difference?

The customer, that's who, Sully was on the hook for $1300.

After an unnecessary argument with my service manager and me, we agreed to meet in my office. We all reviewed the situation. Next we decided to contact the service contract company one last time and plead his case. It seemed futile, as my service advisor had already been in contact with the insurance company numerous times. Sully had been in contact with the insurance company earlier that week. The insurance company had turned my customer against me. They said we were the bad guys. We wanted retail prices to fix his car.

There is nothing wrong with that as we are a car dealer and we are entitled to make a profit. The extended warranty company wanted a discount on the bill. Nope!

So my service manager and I contacted the company once again. We plead his case. The agent on the phone was stalling and making excuses. Finally, we asked for the supervisor. Wouldn't you know it? He was not there. So we left a polite message with our concern and hoped for the best. About two hours later the original agent contacted my service advisor and advised us that the insurance company WOULD pay his entire bill. Sully was elated. He again loves his Audi A8 and will come back to us forever. We made a customer. The moral of the story is not to give up on what you think is right. Secondly, if you are going to purchase an expensive car, go to the brand of dealership you want to purchase. If it is an Audi you want, go to an Audi dealership. Get the MANUFACTURER'S extended warranty. The hassle will be gone from your service. Although this incident turned out great for the customer, they all do not end this way.

QUESTION. Are there Hidden Warranties?

Let's clarify one thing. There is no such thing as a hidden warranty. On the other hand, you can get things paid by the manufacturer outside the warranty period? This is called an after warranty adjustment.

How does this happen? To explain how an after warranty adjustment works, I need to give you some background information

BACKGROUND

Most manufacturers and judges, mind you, look at cars like this. *A vehicle's useful life is 100,000 miles.* Some states, however, have moved that up to 120,000 miles. However, most experts believe a car should last about 100,000 miles. Even though many warranties only cover up to 24,000 of 36,000 miles, most experts believe a car should last 100,000 miles, especially since the lifetime of an engine or transmission is 100,000. If you have a catastrophic failure in that period of mileage, however, you just might be eligible for help from the manufacturer.

This takes into account a few factors. First, are you a good dealership customer? If you have your maintenance performed at the local dealership service department, your chances just went up significantly that the manufacturer would help you.

Businesses want your loyalty. If you are loyal, they will be loyal to you. Understand, that you are not legally entitled to anything, or owed anything more that what the warranty states in writing. However, good loyal owners are eligible for help or assistance from the car manufacturer. If you had your car serviced at your local Ford dealership, chances are that you have bought genuine Ford parts throughout the life of the car. This is another opportunity that Ford Motor Company made money from you. You have earned more loyalty from them. In addition, it is much more likely that the maintenance and service performed on your car was done correctly so there is a better chance that the parts are actually defective, not abused and has not been caused to fail by an independent shop mechanic!

Should that part have failed? Most auto manufacturers want to see the failed parts. This helps them build better vehicles. And sometimes they go back to their vendors and require them to pay for the repairs. It happens.

ANOTHER SCENARIO

Imagine that you have 50,000 or even 90,000 miles on your car. You just may be thinking that it's time to purchase a new one. Who are you going to buy your next car from? The company that took care of you or the evil SOB's that would not help you in a time of need? I suggest you will buy the car from the one who takes care of you in your time of need.

Sometimes when the manufacturer makes an after warranty repair the dealership is required to participate in the cost of that repair. I can tell you as a manager or business owner, I don't like to participate in the cost of a repair if the customer is not loyal to me. If you have been having your car repaired at an independent shop, and now you have a problem; why are you coming to me to solve it?

TOP SECRET

You can get things for free outside the warranty period.

We all want to be heroes and step up in a time of need, but you the customer needs to step to the plate as well. Be loyal to me with your service dollars and when it comes to help, I will be in your corner and fight for you. Again imagine you have 50,000 miles on your car. The car is expected to last 100,000 miles. You can expect some help valuing up to about 50% of the cost. You have received 50% usage of the product. You should get 50% help in many cases. Maybe a little more? Maybe a bit less? The lower the miles, the more the assistance. When you approach the 100k mark, you are hitting the edge of the help line. You have driven what is considered the life of the car.

Make sure you keep a **Record** of all your services. For everyone who moves a lot, or has had a bad experience with a dealership, do not let that interfere with your record keeping. Keep your maintenance records and service your vehicle at a dealership!

TO RECAP…

There are **ABC's** to an After Warranty Adjustment

Do you have **A**LL your service records?

BE a good **C**USTOMER at the **D**EALERSHIP!

TOP SECRET

The auto manufacturer will evaluate your extended warranty purchase to determine if you should receive after warranty assistance.

I have seen numerous customers come in to the service department, outside the warranty period and get help. I experienced a man who drove his Saturn into my service department. His check engine light was flashing. He had over 80,000 miles on the car. I picked up the phone, made a call and he drove out with a brand new catalytic converter. I probably saved him $2000 that day. He called me superman for a long time.

After warranty adjustments happen frequently. There are rules for cooking fish, rules of the road, rules for dating and rules for black jack. In cheating the dealer, I am giving you the rules to save thousands on auto repair. You need to follow the rules for auto repair and you can come up a winner almost every time. Play by the rules and you will win more times than you lose.

5

CAR RENTAL DISCOVERED

You bought your dream car.

The car broke down.

You are getting the car fixed.

Now what?

You need a rental!

Now that your car is in the shop, you need alternative transportation. It is important to understand that every manufacturer does not provide rental coverage. Always ask your sales person to show you the provision in the warranty coverage that states, "You are entitled to a rental vehicle."

Many new car dealers offer this as a courtesy. Understand that this is a benefit offered by the dealership, but certainly not a requirement. Even though this is a "perk" it still costs someone money. If the dealership is paying the bill, recognize this and THANK THEM. This is obviously an attempt to win your loyalty. I have seen dealerships spend thousands of dollars providing cars for customers to drive. Unless your warranty spells this out for you, this is a benefit, not a right!

Some manufactures such as GM provide for a rental car in the event you have a warranty repair needed. Often times they provide up to five days rental coverage. This means you get a free car to drive while your car is in the shop, for 5 days. Other manufacturers do not provide this warranty benefit. Others might contribute to the rental, but not cover the entire bill. This again is spelled out in your owners' or warranty manual. READ THIS AGAIN!!!

Let me walk you through this scenario. You take your car in, you get sent over to the rental agency on site. This is usually a major rental company such as Enterprise Rent A Car. Hertz and some other off brand rental companies have locations at dealerships as well. During this process you will be asked if you would like to take out insurance on the car you are renting.

What should you do?

First, prior to getting your rental or loaner from the dealership, check your own insurance policy. Most major companies have provisions that state you are covered in the event you are driving a rental car. Save your money. This can add up to $10 or more dollars per day that you are in the rental car. Your own insurance may cover an accident. Rental agencies live off your extra money. My suggestion is simple, if you have good coverage from a reputable insurance company, you don't need the insurance. If you're not sure, check with your agent.

TOP SECRET

Your insurance company usually covers you while driving rental car.

If you dent the car while you are driving it, you are responsible. You will pay for the repair. In the likelihood of a dent or ding happening, no problem, turn it in to your insurance they will take care of everything, **except your deductible**! It could also be considered a claim on your record.

THE OPPOSITE SCENARIO (BAD DRIVERS)

If you are a bad driver like me; buy all the insurance you can get from the rental agency. We have almost all heard the comedians talk about driving rental cars and the myths and legends about buying cars from a rental agency. Every single time that I rent a vehicle, I buy the insurance from the rental agency. I am gambling that I will crash the car, bump a pole or run the car off the cliff. And if I do, I am covered. I never worry where I park. I don't care if snow and ice are on the freeways; I am cruising to work. Traffic jam, I can drive down the median. And who cares about potholes. Not me. I bought the insurance. When the clerk at the rental agency walks around and looks at the car, it's not my problem. Go get a rental, buy the insurance, call me and let's do doughnuts in the parking lot tonight.

TOP SECRET

Never drop off your car without a damage inspection.

Upon returning the vehicle, make sure you have the receipt that shows no damage on your car. When you check in and the rental agency is closed, have the dealership service advisor note that there is no damage on the car. I would hate to see you become responsible for damage to the vehicle after you turned it in.

I know very sneaky people who try to turn in cars with damage. They come in after hours and park the car far away from the rental area. They hope that no one sees the damage and for a short time, they get away with it. However, the contract is usually pretty clear. You will be responsible for the damage.

It is illegal for a car rental company to charge a credit card for damages. The rental agreement states that the credit card is used only to secure the rentals and to pay for anything ancillary (upgrades, damage waiver, extra days not covered by dealer) in regards to **renting** the car. Collecting a deductible or charging for damages needs to be an entirely **separate** transaction.

It is also important to understand that that many people think that their credit card will cover them if there is damage. If someone else is paying for the rental (like the dealer) the credit card company will not always step up.

GAS OPTION

As a customer you are required to refill the gas to the level it was when you started. That is fair enough. Even though your car is in the shop, you are responsible for your own gas. I mean you would have to pay for gas in your car. So don't get mad at the rental clerk for that one. And if you don't fill that ride back up; you are in for a treat on your credit card. This treat is hard to swallow. The rental agency will charge you for gas plus other fees.

Should you prepay for gas? This one is a no brainier. The rental agency is charging you a lot more than the going rate for gas. Usually this charge is $2 or more dollars per gallon more than at the station down on the corner. Bottom line; make sure to fill up before you turn the car back into the agency. I only buy the gas option when I am traveling from an airport. Rarely, when I am at the dealership will I purchase this option. There are usually many gas stations very close to the car dealership where I can fill up.

DEPOSIT

TOP SECRET

Never leave the rental agency without your deposit credit.

Rental car deposits are getting kind of sticky now. According to a rental company expert, rental companies rarely take a CHARGE on a real credit card for a replacement rental. They take an authorization, or a hold. The credit card company releases that hold on their own time (usually within 14 days). There is nothing the car rental company can do to release the hold. It falls off in its own time. On a DEBIT card, there is typically an actual CHARGE on the card for security. Upon returning the car, the charge is refunded. Interestingly enough, the banks will process a CHARGE immediately but it usually takes 1-3 days for the REFUND to process. Just be advised, when renting a replacement car, use an actual credit card whenever possible.

The rental agencies are just trying to protect themselves. Deposits are just that. - Deposits. Let me warn you…make sure when you turn in your car; get the receipt that shows they refunded you your money. Never leave the rental agency without your credit receipt.

TOP SECRET
You can get a free upgrade…

Rental car agencies are very similar to car dealers: in fact that they have customer satisfaction ratings as well. I suggest to you that you can get free gas or free upgrades.

Don't be afraid to ask, especially if you are a frequent driver of their cars. You just may drive out in a Caddy. One agency executive I spoke with suggested becoming a member of their club and many times the upgrades would be given without even asking.

If you are paying for the rental yourself, go online and reserve the car. Usually the best deals are online. At least call ahead. I was advised to book a compact car, this way; if the compact car is not available the rental company will upgrade you to a bigger car usually at no cost, or a lesser charge.

6

THE WOMAN CUSTOMER

I am here to tell you women out there, that once you have read this chapter; you will be a master of dealership negotiation. Service Advisors will no longer have the upper hand in your auto repair needs. I am even providing a "cheat sheet" that I have created for you. This tool will save you valuable time and money in your service experience.

Let's start with a great story of one's own personal experience...

I was speaking to an acquaintance recently that owns a BMW. She was telling me of her trials and tribulations of having her car serviced at the BMW dealership and since the dealer price was so expensive, she was going to take the car to an independent repair facility. So naturally, I gave her my, *Cheating the Dealer* Top Secrets on car repair.

A few days later I ran into her at the grocery store and followed up with her experience. Here is what happened:

She contacted the dealership and asked about the price and what exactly did they would do on the service. Was it a manufacturer's recommended service or was it dealership recommended service? Then she contacted the independent repair shop. Guess what, once the comparison was equal, meaning no dealership add on's, just performing what the manufacturer recommended, the price was nearly the same. So why go to the independent shop? **TRUST!** The dealership was charging for additional items that they recommend in the service. Once she got to bottom line of the maintenance, it was an equal scenario.

I cannot promise that no one will ever try to take advantage of you. I am just going to give you the tools and the Top Secret questions to ensure that you are aware of the tricks of the trade.

The question in the above story is not "why is the dealership adding on additional services?" The question is "Why is the independent shop charging the same prices as the dealership for the major service?" This independent shop did not have current factory trained technicians nor were they using BMW Authorized Parts, yet the shop was charging the same price. That to me is a rip off. She saved and so will you!

To answer the other question, "Why is the dealer adding on services to the major service?" They are not good marketers. That dealership was going to overprice a service and lose out on a customer repair. The consumer should not have to point this out, however sometimes it happens.

Did I think she was getting ripped off just because she was a woman?

In this case it was not because she was a woman; it was because both shops were not being compared equally. The dealership was adding on additional repairs and the independent shop was overpricing its labor and parts.

The conventional wisdom is that a woman gets ripped off when she is having her car repaired. I am here to tell you that this does not have to happen.

I have worked in and around 100's of dealerships in my career. I have never trained anyone, consulted at, or managed a store where a male service advisor had as his agenda to take advantage of a woman. If a service sales person is out to get anyone, he is out to get everyone. If you run into someone who you do not trust, stop the transaction. Ask for the manager or leader in the department. Believe me, there will most likely be a woman service advisor or other manager available to correct the situation. If your dealership has a female consultant you can seek her out, too.

Most dealerships have women service advisors just for that situation. And anyone out there if you are considering a career change, ladies this is the job for you. If you love people and are interested in a great career, dealerships want you on staff. Most manufacturers even have specific training classes centered on selling service to women. It is designed for the men who have no clue.

The first place to start is how you are being treated. When was the last time a service advisor shook your hand correctly. Do they make eye contact? Do they treat you as a person? If they do not treat you, as you deserve to be treated, move on to someone else. Most managers are experienced enough to handle this situation. If not find either the General Manager or even the salesperson you bought the car from. It is ridiculous to have to go through things like that; however, it will be worth it. Obviously many dealerships are owned by women and managed by women. I know of many top-performing stores where the Service Manager is a woman. It really blows the men away.

On the other hand, if a man cannot shake your hand firmly, look you in the eye and discuss your car…YOU WIN. He is scared of you. You may as well select the premium package and then ask for it FREE. Did you ever see the Seinfeld episode where Jerry's girlfriend got everything she wanted for free. She was **bold**. She got movie tickets, she avoided speeding tickets, she just asked. I can only imagine when you get your next oil change service. Ask the question. See what you get. And you sure won't get anything unless you do ask. I know that all my dealer buddies are going to go crazy on this story.

I have a close female friend who is a service advisor. When I was the manager, she regularly made as much money or more than I did. She had clients that came for miles and miles to see her. That is the type of service that we all strive to achieve. She could sell better than the male service advisors and the male customers loved her more as much as the female customers. Women flocked to her; many would wait in line to see her. And her customers came to visit like family. Some customers even baked us cookies. She was that good.

Now, I have a young woman who is working for me. When she sells service to men, she just smiles and says to men her now famous line: *"That's not too much money... is it?"* The men quiver and shrink up. "Of course not." they reply, pounding their chest. Men cannot resist a lady's charm. So, turn the tables on us at work. Be charming and beat us at our own game.

Ask a lot of questions regarding your charges up front. Find out how much is the parts and labor itemized. Be bold and confident when you drive your car in the shop. And always read your owners manual. Many of the questions that arise from the repair shop are answered in your owner's manual.

THE ABC'S FOR WOMEN

A. Ask for Itemized List of Repairs

B. Be bold and Confident with the service advisor

C. Check your owner's manual for comparison

D. Dig deep with questions

E. Engage the service advisor in conversation

F. Feel him out

G. Give the authorization or GET OUT!

Ask for an Itemized List of the Repairs

Ethically, legally and it is just good business practice to get an itemized list of necessary repairs. Every dealership repair facility should provide the customer with an itemized list of the repairs needed on the vehicle. As a woman and a customer you have the right to this list.

When you bring your vehicle in for a repair or maintenance concern, the service advisor will ask you for the primary reason for your visit. Once the vehicle has been looked at and the problem has been verified, the dealership service advisor should provide you a written or computer generated list of the repairs necessary for the vehicle. Most dealerships who are modern and customer friendly will provide a type written document. Although this is not a legal and binding document, a typed document will make deciphering the repairs much easier. Most dealerships can fax or email this to you as well.

Be bold and Confident with the service advisor

Ask the service advisor to review this document line by line. There is no shame in not knowing what the heck the service advisor is talking about. Ask for an explanation as you go. Ask for an explanation of each and every line item that he or she is suggesting. A service advisor's job is to educate you on your car. If the service advisor cannot give you the explanation you want, either ask for a manager or leave.

Check your owner's manual for comparison

When it comes to the maintenance on your vehicle, always check in your owner's manual. Ask the service advisor to explain how the dealership services compare with the manufacturer recommended services. Earlier in the maintenance section, I advised that it is ok to recommend items not necessarily noted in the owners manual. However, ask for clarification. Specifically, ask "is this service recommended by the car manufacturer?" If yes. OK. If the answer is no then probe further.

Dig deep with questions

Ask the service advisor why does this part need to be replaced? Ask, "Did the part in question fail?" Or ask, "Did the part need to be replaced for maintenance?" More questions that you could answer are:

- Does the manufacturer recommend this service?
- How long can I go without replacing this part?
- If I don't have it replaced or serviced, what are the consequences?
- What does that part do exactly?

Another couple of great questions to ask the service advisor are: How long have you worked here? How long have you worked for this brand? Understanding how long the person has worked at the dealership will also help determine how much of a stake in your satisfaction that service person has. Is this person committed to your long-term satisfaction? Service Advisors that move from store to store are not the ones that have your best interest at heart. Look for the men or women that are there day in and day out. I have one man who has been with the company nearly twenty years. He is the go to person for everyone, including women. They truly trust him with their cars. He is the guy that gives you the inside scoop on your car and what you can get away with not doing today. This is the person you want to build a relationship with.

Engage the service advisor in conversation

Pretend it's a first date. I encourage you to develop a relationship with your service advisor. This relationship is hopefully going to last for years. You should trust that service person explicitly. The trust that you build starts immediately and it is truly up to the service advisor to cultivate the relationship. Be open to his advice. It is always good to have a go to person when it comes to repairs, especially in the beginning of the relationship. That's why *Cheating The Dealer* is so important. Utilize the questions I have spelled out. You will be the master of the conversation. Once the trust is developed you can feel at ease that the dealership is going to serve you right.

I suggest you ask my favorite question. "Would you replace this on your car? Or, "If your wife owned this car, would you spend your money on servicing this component?" **<u>The correct answer is self-explanatory.</u>**

Give the authorization or GET OUT!

When you feel you have the necessary information, give the approval or get the hell out of there. If you are not 100% confident that the service advisor is honest and truthful, ask for the manger or find a new dealership for repairs.

I stand by my original points that most advisors are honest and truthful; it's still your car and your money. I never give anyone my hard earned money without knowing and believing what is being said to me. Or I should say, sold to me. And make them sell you on it. Make them treat you the way you want to be treated. Make them educate you on how your car works.

If you pay money to my dealership or anyone else's dealership I want you to feel good about it. I want you to say, that service advisor did a great job. If you do not get that warm and fuzzy feeling, don't buy it.

MY SURVEY

As a man in a man's world of cars my view of the industry gets blurred now and then about the feelings of women towards the dealership. I sometimes get drawn into believing that everyone should believe what I believe and just come right in and have his or her car serviced. It is obvious to me and I sometimes think it should be to you. That is the problem in itself.

I asked myself, "How do women think about auto repair?" How do women, I wonder, perceive the word dealership? Do woman enjoy spending time at the dealership? Do they like or dislike the entire service experience? I had to know the answers to these questions. I have many more, too. I decided to email many women friends and acquaintances and ask a few poignant questions about my world, the new car dealership. I was quite astonished as to how they answered and responded to my survey.

I wanted to find out how you as a woman felt before, during and after a service visit.

I sent out emails to women in an age range from twenty-one to sixty something. The women had education levels between high school and a master's degree. Some were stay at home moms and others were insurance agents, sales women, marketing women, business owners and other high-level executives. So I would say that I had a cross reference of women in my survey. I have quite the sample of women in my group.

Before Visiting the Dealership

It was most important to understand how many felt about the word dealership. Most women I surveyed dreaded the word dealership. Words like time consuming, overbearing men, and intimidating were words that many women used in describing the new car dealership. One woman described the dealership as sterile. YIKES! It is no wonder why as a single man I do not make points on a date by informing my potential mate that I manage a car dealership. This was definitely good information to know. Sterile conjures up some really nasty imaginations.

Many felt like they were going to be treated differently because they are women. Most women assumed that they were going to be taken advantage of. It is almost as if you are preparing for a battle when you head to main street motors. This should not be the case in the dealership repair world. You should get that warm and fuzzy feeling from your dealership. You should really feel like a client. I want you to feel the professional atmosphere that most dealerships strive to achieve. I know that the dealer principal wants you to experience a family like atmosphere. Many are working hard to ensure this for you. This is a trust issue as well. Once that trust is created, you will be able to let down your armor. Having the information to verify your service persons behavior will allow you to lower your guard. Look for consistency in the processes the dealerships follow. You should get treated the same way every time you visit the store.

Not surprising the results from women who had experience with the automotive industry. These women were insurance agents marketing representatives and a few sales women. They were slightly more educated on the buying and negotiating process. The more familiar with the actual dealership and its techniques, the more comfortable the women were having their car serviced.

This is the most important secret I can reveal. The more familiar one is with the dealership practices, the better experience they will have.

TOP SECRET

The more familiar one is with the dealership practices, the better experience they will have.

It all boils down to education and knowledge of the dealership world. This is exactly the reason for reading *Cheating the Dealer.* This read will give you the advantage when negotiating with the service sales person. This is the insight you need when dealing with the service department. This read should make you feel more comfortable in dealing with a car dealer person.

What services need to be done?

I also found that most women would like to know "what services need to be done" to the car at the appropriate time and mileage. Earlier in the book I shared a sample maintenance chart. Also, keep your owners manual close at hand. Utilize this while you are in the dealership. This will service as your bible and trust meter. The owner's manual tells you exactly what needs to be completed on your car at the exact intervals. The service person should quote your needs based upon the manufacturer's recommendation.]

Add On Repairs?

Some stated, it is the "ad on'" that I worry about. Remember that some of the ADD ON's are ok as long as they are **_not_** included in the package. The dealership should advise you of exactly what is necessary to meet the manufacturers recommended requirements. Then they should identify the additional maintenance items to ensure the maximum reliability for your car. Once you have this broken out into an itemized list, the fear factor should be reduced.

You can now start asking those questions on the *cheat sheet*. Take each item one at a time and make the service advisor review them with you. You will walk away as an educated consumer. You will walk away with your car maintained to the manufacturer recommendation. You will fulfill the warranty requirements.

Then you should you maintain your car-To your level of care. The "ADD ON" services should make you feel like you are maximizing the performance of your car to YOUR standards. Make sure you are presented the facts listed in order of importance, safety, primary concern, failed items, maintenance and other items. This will ensure you get the comfort level you need.

I love my car!

I know of many women who love their cars. They love to go fast. They know more about their Porsche than I do. They love the big fat tires on the back of their Mustang GT. They maintain their car to a different level than I would. I also know moms who routinely change their oil more times than the manufacturer requires them to perform this service. They always request a brake check at each interval and when the pads get down to a certain discard usage, (let's say 50% worn) they want the brake pads replaced. It is her discretion on how to maintain the minivan or sports car. I advise my service advisors to provide the information and allow them to choose the services that provide them the highest level of security for their own car. This is the level of knowledge you can have by asking proper questions.

Honey You Do It.

Most of the women I interviewed were not too interested in visiting the dealership. They preferred to have their husband or male friend take care of the car repairs. Most felt as if the dealership would keep their car for hours if not days even on simple repairs.

Throughout my surveys I got the sense that most women are willing to service the car at the dealership if they knew the dealer had a very good customer satisfaction rating. This is another top secret from the book. Your customer satisfaction is very important to the dealership. Just knowing that your opinions will actually drive women business into or away from the dealership is a powerful lesson for all of us.

DURING THE DEALERSHIP VISIT

The results were similar on the survey concerning the actual service visit. The act of negotiating over the repairs and maintenance that made many women feel overwhelmed. Many did not know what exactly the repair was that the service advisor was suggesting or how much she should pay for the item. One woman shared with me how she just tries to act as if she understands. Imagine how she will feel once she truly has a thorough understanding of the repair process.

How are prices computed?

Another discovery that I learned was that women want to know how prices are determined. As you may remember from earlier section of *Cheating the Dealer* we covered how the dealership service department determines the price of a repair. Actually you can request that the service advisor show you in the labor time manual how they calculated the repair estimate. Only in this section do I reveal this top secret.

TOP SECRET
You can request the service advisor to show you in the labor time manual how the estimate was calculated.

Most dealerships follow a strict guideline utilizing this labor manual. Ask the service advisor to show you the labor time standard manual he or she used to calculate this estimate. They should be able to go to the exact page and section where the time is documented. If they do this, you can trust this person. You are assured that they are using an industry standard for pricing or repairs.

You may also ask to see the car in the shop. Ask the service person to escort you to the car and point out the defective parts. Ask the mechanic the same questions. Make sure the mechanic and the service advisor are saying the same thing. Remember the mechanic may speak a bit more technical that the service guy, he will try to help you understand the car as well.

Trust is the Key

Throughout this chapter and in the entire book, I am dwelling on the trust issue. You will need to ask those questions that I laid out earlier in this section to ensure you received the best deal. It is important to use your instinct to determine whether the service salesperson is treating you fairly. Asking questions like is this for "repair" or "maintenance" will help you determine whether or not to part with your money. "How long can I go without this item?" These types of questions can aide in your determination of the trust of the service person. Do not be afraid to seek counsel from the manager of the dealership. That person is specifically hired to ensure that you are satisfied. The service manager should tell you the ins and outs on your car.

Many of the women who were in the business or related business understood how hard most car dealerships work to cater to women customers. Like most business it boils down to each individual service advisor that they meet. Nearly all of these women suggested to other women to deal with the woman on the service drive if possible. They try just a bit harder to make you feel comfortable in the repair and maintenance process.

AFTER THE DEALERSHIP VISIT

Whether it was the sales process or the service process most of the women suggested that they were not really sure if they were given the best prices or possibly they could have received a better deal.

The time to worry about this is before the repairs have been authorized. Once the repairs are complete it is too late to be concerned about the price. Once the repairs are authorized and completed, your negotiating power is greatly reduced. You have no legal standing to go back to the service advisor and ask for a discount. You have already agreed and the work is done.

Price shopping after the work is done will get you nowhere but mad. As a marketing person, if a consumer is fixated on price, that is the easiest objection to overcome. If a consumer is shopping after the fact and looking to make a change in shops; I say welcome to my arena. Quoted prices are easy to undercut. I can meet or beat anyone's deal. If you call me and ask about a price for a certain part and tell me how much you paid, I can always beat that price. It is a game of the mind at this point. The time to be concerned is before the repairs are completed.

Each and every female car person I spoke with had one similar piece of advice: Always research and ask questions before giving the go-ahead on the repairs. Do not give the approval until you understand what you are paying to have repaired or serviced.

THE PERSPECTIVE OF FEMALE DEALERSHIP EMPLOYEES

After gaining insight to the female perspective on their opinion of the new car dealership, I went into the dealership as well. I sampled opinions of women working in the dealership too. Many were young women starting out their careers as cashiers and clerks on up to women at all age ranges and all levels of their lives. Some of the participants were writing service, service managers, and even general managers of the dealership. So as I sat down with a few female auto dealership service people. I wanted to gain their perspective on the business that I love. I suggest they are a good sample of women feelings around the country towards the new car dealership service department. I wanted to be able to pass along their advice to you. My results were nothing short of intriguing.

Women in the dealership mostly had empathy for the females that bring their cars in the shop. Most women try harder with women clients. They try to let the female customers know that it is perfectly acceptable that they do not know all the technical information about their vehicle.

The women service advisors try just a bit harder to make the women feel comfortable. They have empathy towards the female consumer. Most said they work to overcome the armor that most women have towards the male dominated business. One female service advisor told me that she advises women not to say "NO", "just to say NO". She advises to learn what is going on with your car. Learn by asking the important questions as spelled out here in *Cheating the Dealer.*

One woman in particular makes it a point to spell out *in detail* the needs of the car. She says, "Women are visual" they need to see it on paper. This helps them understand and prioritize the repairs and maintenance. She also agrees with the method of laying out the necessary items based upon Safety First, Primary Item Second and on through the list. Most women, she says would rather know how to maintain their vehicles from a safety stand point then how to keep the vehicle on the road longer.

They also said to always seek to build a relationship with your service advisor. Let them know that you are open to the dealership suggestions. Let the service advisor know what your budget is during the conversation. Most service advisors (especially the female advisors) are honest and will work to meet your needs.

I asked women service advisors for their thoughts on the male dominated business. Many informed me that there still is some men that think women are an easy mark in the service driveway. Each one told me that their best advice was to be educated on the questions to ask. Make sure you request, even demand, a full detail and itemized list for the vehicle. The dealer should do this for you each and every time. They should do this at Zero Cost. It should always be complimentary. There are now companies that specialize in this and offer software to the dealership to assist them in presenting options to the consumer.

According to the female service advisors, many male service advisors would offer discounts to women in an effort to win their favor. This was purely an ego driven situation. The men want to be the go to guy for you, the woman. It makes the men feel better; especially if you are attractive. We all have seen the clips of beauty and the geek. My geek service advisors want to be your guy at the dealership. And I am sure they will work hard to earn your respect and trust. Occasionally this does require them to give you a discount. HA, you win!

Overwhelmingly the women service advisors suggested to all women that they should seek out the women at the dealership whenever possible. Most suggested that the women want to provide a better service.

And finally they all agreed that the dealership was the place for women to have their car serviced. You can be assured in the dealership that there is always a higher power to present your case to as well. There are the managers, the directors and finally the Dealer herself that can be the judge of your needs in a case where it could be overwhelming. Also the dealership wants you to return for not only service but for the next new car purchase. The dealership has a long-term stake in your satisfaction.

Just a word of caution from the ladies: even though you have a woman service person, she is still a sales person and do not just let your guard down on the first visit. Make her earn your trust too. Make her present your needs to you in the way you want to hear them.

Reading this section gave you the necessary tools and knowledge to keep your car maintained to your level. You now have the information you need to be secure that YOU will not be ripped off. You have the proper questions to ask the service person. You now have your equivalent to a Master's Degree in auto dealership service negotiations.

Tear out the *Cheat Sheet* and carry this with you at all times. When you find yourself in the dealership situation; pull this card out and collect the information you need to make that educated decision. You will show up at the dealership with problems and walk away with the store. You will have the men eating out of your hands. I suggest that they will even respect you for your taking the time to become and educated consumer.

The next time one of your friends has doubts about taking the car to the shop just tell them that you "Cheat the Dealer" all the time. Tell them how you love to go into the store and win every time you visit. I suggest you tell your hubby or male friend that from now on you will be handling the auto repair. And loving it!

ADVICE FROM THE EXPERTS

I asked a few prominent friends in the business for their advice for you. Below is a copy of the email I sent out along with the responses.

-----Original Message-----
From: Steven Shaw [mailto:mydealercoach@gmail.com]
Sent: Thursday, February 12, 2009 10:40 AM
Subject: RE: Advice

Everyone,

Imagine you were giving advice to a friend, your sister or mother. What advice would you tell them to make sure they get the best experience at the dealership

Thanks for your help

Steve Shaw

Just Be Honest

"I suggest that when you have a problem, just be honest with us. I would rather take care of someone who is honest and humble, especially someone who asks for help. I will break my back for the person. I will give them my time for free both as a mechanic and manager for someone who deserves it. Verses the person who lies and tries to cover their tracks just to get something for free."

Tim Thomas, Service Manager. Audi Dealership

The Meeting and Greeting

I do not think that it is up to the customer to have a great experience, but it is up to us to start out on the right track. Remember the three things that happen during a greeting:

Trust is formed

Value judgments are made

The mood is set

For both the customer and the dealer, trust is the most important thing that can happen in the meeting and greeting.

Hal Makorow, General Manager – Ford Dealership

<u>What should I do?</u>

I just bought a car and I am having a problem with it. What should I do? "Modern vehicles are completely computerized. Do you want to take it to an independent and have them take a "stab at it"? When you take it to the dealer, you know that someone who has been properly trained will be working on your vehicle. They have years of training and are constantly being re-trained. They have the necessary equipment to repair your vehicle. The other option is a mechanic that works on many different vehicles and is not specialized on one particular vehicle."

I took my vehicle to the dealer and I am having difficulty with my service advisor. What should I do? "If you are having difficulty understanding and/or dealing with your service advisor, don't just get angry and take your vehicle elsewhere. The dealership wants, actually needs your business. Talk to your service advisors' supervisor (i.e. service manager). He/she is there to handle any issues you have with your vehicle or problems you are having with dealer personnel. They are there to help you and to find a solution. A majority of the time it is just a misunderstanding or lack of communication. ENT your frustrations but don't be rude. You treat people the way you want to be treated— I know - cliché!"

Robert Sikiyan, Service Advisor – Porsche Dealership

Be Loyal

These are my tips to my family and friends:

- Look for a dealership that offers some sort of reward program - points, free oil changes, free loan car, etc.

- **Stick to the manufacturer's maintenance requirements** - do you really drive in severe conditions?

- Ask for a breakout of individual services - **Itemized List**

- Buy only extra services that the advisor can demonstrate value

- **Ask for a discount** - bring in advertised prices for same services

- **Stay loyal** - expect superior service and treatment

- Give a good survey, even if things don't go as smooth as planned

- Ask for the manager and calmly explain what happened and what your expectations were

Perry Phillips, Fixed Operations Director
– Multi Franchise Dealership

Meet the Family

I try to go out of my way to make my customers feel like they are a part of the family. When you leave my dealership you will feel like you have been here for years even on a first visit.

Frank Parra, Service Advisor - Ford Dealer

Great Advice

A couple things I recommend a customer should know about when visiting a dealership and how to know if they got the best service.

- Make sure the service advisor makes eye contact

- The service advisor should greet you with a smile and offer a handshake along with their name

- The service advisor should try to find out what brings you into the dealership today

- The service advisor should make your main concern the first line on the repair order

- The service advisor should repeat to you the concerns you have identified to ensure he / she understands why you are here

- The service advisor should schedule a time to call you with the diagnosis

- The service advisor should review any charges with you before you leave when you drop you car off

- The service advisor should itemize the repair order for you when completed

- The service advisor should review the entire repair order when you pick up the vehicle

- The service advisor should make sure you are completely satisfied before you leave the dealership

Chuck E. Moore, Service Manager – Ford Dealership

If all else fails

My advice that I would tell a loved one who is going to a dealership is simple:

Pay close attention to the service advisor you deal with. Make sure the advisor listens to what you are requesting. If the advisor begins to recommend or suggests any services or repairs that are needed for your vehicle, ask why you need this repair.

If you do not understand any of the specifics that your advisor gives to you, ask him questions. Do not rush into any sale! For any decision you make, do not give into any sale. Go home and do research on how much on average a specific repair costs.

If all else fails, call me.

Dwayne Granguillhome, Service Advisor
– Ford Dealership

We Appreciate You

When I was a service advisor, I always preferred that when a customer has a problem, that he or she would be honest with me and tell me the real issues. This way I can determine the best course of action up front. I understand that customers often have problems and they are worried that the service person is going to rip them off. In almost every scenario it is the relationship that carries us through. The key element in the service industry is establishing a trust with one another. I always took the extra steps to build a relationship with my customers.

It does not matter which position we hold; it is that bond that we build with our owners that will ensure a lasting connection. Now as a dealership consultant, I teach my clients the importance of building this relationship. As I am an agent of change and my company directs change in dealerships, we never lose sight of the true customer, the person who comes in our service departments and pays the bills. It is your car and your money. We are responsible for your happiness. We appreciate the opportunity to service you.

Dave Vaden, Consultant, M5 Management Services

The Bottom Line is Trust

Build a relationship with your Service Advisor. He/she is the most important person in the dealership, as far as a customer is concerned. Become known by your Service Advisor and seek to actually know them. It is that kind of relationship that will assure the following:

You will have a much better chance of getting a good deal on all your services and you will be sold only those services you really need.

The Advisor will become acquainted with your vehicle and your driving habits. This will help him/her accurately schedule your service intervals and make sure your vehicle will be available to you on a timely manner.

Not only will all your service records be in one place but the person who knows your history (and you) will be there as well. This is invaluable if you ever need financial assistance from the manufacturer or from the dealer.

When it is time to purchase your next vehicle, your Service Advisor is valuable source of information. He/she can help you decide which vehicle that would best suit your needs and he/she can introduce you to a Sales Person that they trust to take good care of you.

The real bottom line is the word TRUST. A real relationship, built over time, that has survived good days and bad will establish a bond of trust. In the end that trust will give you something we all seek, peace of mind. What a great feeling to have one less thing to worry about!

Bob Cawley, Service and Parts Director,
Multi Franchise Dealership Group

Ditto

You can read above from some men and women that I highly respect in the industry a reoccurring theme -TRUST. We want to build a relationship with you. We want you to feel comfortable and if I dare say so, a part of our family. As men and women in the automotive field we work very hard every day to build that trust. It does work both ways. We will be upfront and honest with you, please do the same with us.

As the professionals above suggest, tell us the real problem. Explain that you left your emergency brake on while going down the Rocky Mountains. It helps us correctly diagnose your problem or concern. It will lead us in the correct direction to maximize your savings.

Since this entire book is my quote, I'll just say DITTO to all of the wisdom sent over by those professionals.

7

HOW TO ENSURE A GREAT EXPERIENCE

In any business, customers wanted to feel satisfied. Exponentially, customers want better service and satisfaction based on the amount of money they spend. This is critical with car purchases and service because of the hefty price tags.

So, what should you do if you do not feel you are treated as you would like in the dealership? What should you expect from the staff? How should you get the satisfaction you deserve?

In a dealership there is a chain of command. As I covered in previous chapters, starting with the service advisor / salesman and moving on through the service manager and finally the general manager; when things go wrong, follow the chain. Usually someone will be there to help out. Even though staff at the dealership gets extremely busy in their daily routine; a customer complaint is the last thing they want!

Most good managers will take time out and resolve the issue. Don't be afraid to ask for what you want. A good manager will reasonably sort out the issue and make good judgment on the outcome. I am not saying that it's always free; usually the problem can be mitigated.

My philosophy is to solve the concern like this... Always Be Considerate, ABC...

- **Always seek to understand the concern**
- **Be open to determine the correct course of action**
- **Consider how the cost is going to paid**

A solution is always available!

TYPES OF DEALERSHIP SOLUTIONS

Many times the dealership is responsible; an example would be a "comeback" or "recheck." A comeback is simply when your car comes back to the dealership for a repair that should have been done correctly the first time. If we as the dealership did something that is not right, we will typically accept responsibility.

Many times these comeback issues are related to the description of the problem that the service advisor wrote down on the repair order. This is another reason why your service advisor should be competent and have great listening skills.

Many times, the dealership will just take care of the second repair or "comeback."

Occasionally there is a shared responsibility for both the customer and the dealership. A shared responsibility could result in a split of the cost of the repair. In this option, dealers look for the customer to pay for the parts and the dealer will pay the labor. Sometimes a three way split is in order, the dealer, the customer and the manufacturer. I suggest that you be open to these options.

Most dealers will offer a compromise, as this is good customer service. Another reason is if you go to court, the judge will look for the company offer. If the dealer has dug his feet in and not helped, many judges look unfavorable on this situation. Can you imagine a judge that has not had car trouble? If the dealer makes a reasonable offer, you should take it. Imagine getting 50% off? Pat yourself of the back and take the rest of your money to the bank.

A DEALER IS A FRANCHISE

It is critical to understand how the dealer relates to the manufacturer when considering customer service and satisfaction. Most new car dealerships are franchises. The auto manufacturer chooses a corporation or person to run the franchise. Each is independently owned and operated. Dealerships administer the manufacturer's warranty and they are responsible to administer the warranty honestly and with integrity. Car dealership service departments fix cars. Once the repair is completed, the dealership must submit a warranty claim to the automaker. Dealers do have to be accountable for all of the claims they submit to the manufacturer for reimbursement. Sometimes it is possible for a dealer to submit a claim and it gets rejected from the manufacturer.

Other times, the manufacturer will audit the dealership claims and find the claim did not meet the requirements and the dealership has to give the money back.

An example would be, if the dealership diagnosed a problem and replaced a component. The component was then returned to the builder and then found to be in working condition; the dealership must return the money for the part and the labor. It happens. The consumer is not responsible, just the dealer. At the independent shop, the consumer pays for the miss-diagnosis. That happens too!

There are companies who are charged with evaluating the Auto Manufacturers Customer Satisfaction Index or CSI. Each manufacturer, such as General Motors, Ford, Toyota, and Nissan grades its own dealerships on its customer satisfaction. Typically each dealership gets graded on your experience with your salesman, whether you would come back to buy another car or if you would recommend that your friend buy a car.

The same philosophy applies to the service department as well. Were you happy with your service advisor? Did they fix your car the first time? Will you recommend this service department to you friend?

It is a big deal to us. Many times the manufacturers pay money to car dealers based upon CSI rankings and scores. Many times sales people and service people get paid on how well they treat their customers.

In no way am I suggesting you hold this over the dealerships head, however, you are in command when it comes to warranty service. The dealership should always treat you with courtesy and respect. The dealership should provide you with everything we have talked about so far. They should be happy to do this for you. Never forget you are the consumer and we not only want you to be happy, we need you to tell everyone you are Completely Satisfied, or Extremely Satisfied. Anything less than the top box or the highest score is a failure grade for us at a dealership. If you cannot give everyone the highest grade naturally, then we want to know about it. And we will do whatever (as long as it's legal) to make it right and make you happy.

I remember my neighbor bought a new Ford Mustang from the dealership here in California. For whatever reason, this model did not come with rear floor mats. She discovered this and was slightly disappointed that a brand new Ford did not have floor mats in the rear. After calling the dealer, she was told that for about $50 bucks she could have rear floor mats.

A few days after she purchased the car, it broke down on the side of the road, a Friday night of course. She ended up towing the car in that night after hours. She caught a cab to her dinner plans and then a cab home. The next day was Saturday and she caught me outside and told me the story. I explained to her that she could get her cab paid for both ways and I bet she would be getting free floor mats soon.

The manufacturer was sending out its sales satisfaction survey to her. My advice was to call her salesman and ask him about the survey, explain about the break down and politely mention to him that she was more than unhappy about the ability to carry anyone in the rear of her car because she had no floor mats. We all know where this is going. The salesman immediately went to his manager, bought her some mats, installed them in the back seat area and she picked up her car from the service with the minor repair completed, the floor mats and a check for the exact amount of the cab ride. Naturally she was now completely satisfied and told everyone to shop at this Ford store.

I teach my service advisors the importance of customer satisfaction. I also teach them to remind the customer how important it is to grade them at the highest levels. Although I never outright paid a customer for a good grade, I know many people who do this. Some dealerships will give a customer a free tank of gas to either return the survey completed with all A's. Or others have been known to give free oil changes for the best score. Each and every dealership is different when it comes to Customer Satisfaction. For every business, taking care of customers is truly the key to longevity and success.

I do know of many very successful car dealer owners who have tried to get other franchises and were denied because their current customer satisfaction ratings were not up to standards.

Please don't try to go overboard when it comes to this ACE Card. Everyone has his or her limits.

Remember the chain of command or chain of customer satisfaction again.

- Service Advisor
- Service Manager

- Parts and Service Director
- General Manager
- Dealer Principal

It is usually best to speak to the service manager before calling the manufacturer. Many times the manufacturer turns around and calls the dealership.

On certain issues, especially technical issues you can request that a manufactures representative meet you. Sometimes a Field Service Engineer can come and look at your car. These engineers are mechanics who have special training with the vehicle and usually have access to the engineers who designed the car. They can get directions and answers that the dealership mechanics are not able to access.

In the good ole days, the automakers representatives were readily available to meet and discuss cars with consumers. Today, the manufacturers have less staff and time to meet customers. Dealership service managers many times have been called upon to negotiate resolutions to customer problems.

Many dealership service managers have authority to offer warranty assistance. These service managers have very strict guidelines to follow. However if you fall within those guidelines, you will find a potential for large cost savings.

Typically to request an after warranty adjustment, you will need to speak with the service manager or higher. Occasionally you will have to speak with a representative from the manufacturer. All the automakers have a customer service centers to assist with customer concerns.

DEALERSHIP CUSTOMER SATISFACTION RATINGS AND YOU

It is important to me that when you shop at my store or any dealership, I want you to be happy. There are actually three levels of customer satisfaction that most of us strive to achieve. This especially applies to the woman car buyer or repair buyer. Making a recommendation to another for purchases is a highly coveted or scared act.

Many business or repair facilities can achieve the first level, which is *satisfaction*. You brought your car into the shop and they completed the services at the level you expected. The second level is return. Are you willing to return to that facility for repairs? And the final level is your reference. Are you willing to put your name on a shop? Do you feel comfortable suggesting to others that this dealership will take care of your friends as well as they took care of you? That is the level most dealerships strive for and that you should accept.

We all live in a customer service driven world. Those of us in a service industry live and die by our customer satisfaction.

Customers hold the power. Your opinion counts for lot more than just free words. Many times our paychecks depend on your satisfaction. We work hard to make our world, our dealership, and the best place for you and your car repair.

We may fail to call at the proper time. We may fail to fix the car right the first time. Occasionally, we may not have that part in stock to fix your car today. We will make it up to you. We do, however, want you to return. Usually we don't mind you calling our bosses to let them know the good and bad of your experience. Many people would just walk away. We want to know you are happy. We want your concerns voiced and we especially want you to honestly check the box completely satisfied with service and definitely recommend us to your friends.

Once the car repair is complete, I suggest you focus on your satisfaction with the service advisor. Ask yourself these questions now:

1. Did the service advisor spend the necessary time with you to make an educated decision?

2. Or did you feel rushed?

3. Was your car completed in the time frame that it was promised?

4. Were the repairs completed to your satisfaction?

    This simply means, the car was broke – is it fixed now? One day later? One week later? One month later?

5. Did this dealership make you want to return for future visits?

6. Finally, could you put your reputation out there and tell a woman friend how satisfied you are with Hometown Motors?

These are the real determining factors on your satisfaction. You spent the time to understand the deal. You educated yourself on the proper services to be completed. You spent your money wisely. You have assurance that the car will last at least until the next visit.

The manufacturer may send you a survey via mail, email or telephone;

- *Are you completely satisfied?*
- *Will you definitely recommend the dealership to your friends and colleagues?*

I hope you can answer a resounding yes to these two questions. If not I beg you to go to your servicing dealer and advise someone. Anyone! Let them know that you were not treated the way you wanted to be treated. The service manger, general manager or even dealer owner will listen to you. Especially now, they know based on my survey of women that you will have your car maintained at their dealership if they have good satisfaction ratings. It sounds like a winner all the way around to me.

Now go and enjoy this peace of mind. If you are one of the people who truly love your car, I am excited that you made these smart decisions. Go tear up the road for the next 3, 6, 12 months. See you next time. If you are a person who uses their car as just utility and a means to get around, go enjoy your savings. Keep the money you saved for something special.

Finally, after all these lessons, rules and checklists, you are poised to save thousands of dollars over the life of your car. I have taught you and provided examples of the questions to ask the service advisor during the negotiations. I have given you the tools you need to ensure you will never get ripped off from any new car dealership. In fact you will save thousands on your auto repair from now on! As of today The Top Secrets of the Dealership world are out there. They are no longer classified. Today you have your masters' degree in saving money at the new car dealership; you are an educated consumer, you are:

CHEATING THE DEALER!

The End of the book, the beginning of savings...

At the Dealership!

BUY A SHARE OF THE FUTURE IN YOUR COMMUNITY

These certificates make great holiday, graduation and birthday gifts that can be personalized with the recipient's name. The cost of one S.H.A.R.E. or one square foot is $54.17. The personalized certificate is suitable for framing and will state the number of shares purchased and the amount of each share, as well as the recipient's name. The home that you participate in "building" will last for many years and will continue to grow in value.

Here is a sample SHARE certificate:

HABITAT FOR HUMANITY

THIS CERTIFIES THAT

YOUR NAME HERE

HAS INVESTED IN A HOME FOR A DESERVING FAMILY

1985-2005

TWENTY YEARS OF BUILDING FUTURES IN OUR COMMUNITY ONE HOME AT A TIME

1200 SQUARE FOOT HOUSE @ $65,000 = $54.17 PER SQUARE FOOT
This certificate represents a tax deductible donation. It has no cash value.

YES, I WOULD LIKE TO HELP!

I support the work that Habitat for Humanity does and I want to be part of the excitement! As a donor, I will receive periodic updates on your construction activities but, more importantly, I know my gift will help a family in our community realize the dream of homeownership. **I would like to SHARE in your efforts against substandard housing in my community!** *(Please print below)*

PLEASE SEND ME _____ SHARES at $54.17 EACH = $ $_____

In Honor Of: _____

Occasion: (Circle One)   HOLIDAY   BIRTHDAY   ANNIVERSARY

    OTHER: _____

Address of Recipient: _____

Gift From: _____ *Donor Address:* _____

Donor Email: _____

I AM ENCLOSING A CHECK FOR $ $_____ PAYABLE TO HABITAT FOR HUMANITY <u>OR</u> PLEASE CHARGE MY VISA OR MASTERCARD *(CIRCLE ONE)*

Card Number _____ Expiration Date: _____

Name as it appears on Credit Card _____ Charge Amount $ _____

Signature _____

Billing Address _____

Telephone # Day _____ Eve _____

PLEASE NOTE: Your contribution is tax-deductible to the fullest extent allowed by law.
Habitat for Humanity • P.O. Box 1443 • Newport News, VA 23601 • 757-596-5553
www.HelpHabitatforHumanity.org

CPSIA information can be obtained at www.ICGtesting.com

227694LV00002B/6/P